Leadership for Social Change and Development

"This is a must read for anyone seeking to explore their true purpose in life, or wishing to discover from within the multiple dynamics that have shaped their individual experience. With practical guidance and illuminating case studies, the book offers a unique journey of personal discovery that will guide readers on a path towards greater inner peace."

—Gareth Owen OBE, *Humanitarian Director, Save the Children UK International, London*

"This new book by Cornelia Walther invites us to travel the path to change in our own lives and that of the communities and societies in which we live, considering the aspirational, emotional, cognitive, and physiological dimensions. Those who work with people, as well as who teach and study this topic need to read this book!"

—Graciela Tonon, *Professor of Quality of Life and Research Methodology, Universidad de Palermo, Argentina, Buenos Aires, Argentina*

"This book is a gift, because it is a reminder that no matter how small the step forward, if done mindfully, deliberately nurturing a compassion for self and others, we can model a way of being in relation to our surroundings that will nurture in others a respect for the collective good. Our journey begins and ends alone, but we influence and are influenced by our environment, why not then, take every opportunity to shape it in such a way that it feeds the soul. Apparently, there are many of us out there that have the same idea. What fun it would be to meet up!

Holding this book in my hand, it is like having found not one, but many friends that I have yet to meet. Life is such a gift but oftentimes we become bogged down in the daily struggle of daily deadlines and deliverables that we forget the promise we made to ourselves to affect a positive change in the world. This toil gradually extends into years and decades until suddenly we are jolted back (if we are lucky) to the possibility that indeed there is more, and that the change is not outside of ourselves but in how we relate to ourselves and the world around us. That ember of hope is a spark, that if nurtured, can allow us to evolve into our highest selves and thereby become the change we thought could only be found externally, either through our vocation or by seeking inspiration from others."

—Marielle Sander, *UNFPA Representative, Port Moresby, Papua New Guinea*

Cornelia C. Walther

Leadership for Social Change and Development

Inspiration and Transformation

palgrave
macmillan

Cornelia C. Walther
Tübingen, Germany

ISBN 978-3-030-76224-7 ISBN 978-3-030-76225-4 (eBook)
https://doi.org/10.1007/978-3-030-76225-4

This Palgrave Macmillan imprint is published by the registered company Springer Nature Switzerland AG
The registered company address is: Gewerbestrasse 11, 6330 Cham, Switzerland

Acknowledgment

I began this book with the timid hope of finding a handful of individuals who do not only have an inspiring story, but who are willing to share it. I found more than I dreamt to hope for. What you are holding in your hands is the result of beautiful people who generously share a glimpse of their journey of being and becoming, with us. I am grateful to all of them. Over the past years many others have shared their thoughts and time with me, helping me see, learn, and grow. I am thankful to all of them.

Furthermore, I thank my parents, Barbara and Manfred Walther for being who they are and were, influencing thereby who I am and become. I am thankful for the unfailing support and professionalism experienced by all members of Palgrave Macmillan, in particular my amazing editors Alina Yurova and Ann-Katrin Bircher whose availability and openness allowed this book to happen; as well as Henry Rogers and Arun Kumar Anbalagan for their expertise during the publication processing.

Finally, I am indebted to You, for giving this book a chance of contributing to your life. This book represents a small fraction of the growing community of likeminded thinkers and doers that is expanding whilst you read these lines. If the words and thoughts, the stories, and questions on the following pages resonate with You, making you feel at home, you are part of this community.

Please get in touch via LinkedIn: https://www.linkedin.com/in/corneliawalther

or using via the Contact section on https://www.poze.cc

Cornelia C. Walther

Introduction

This book illustrates, through lived stories, how our being and becoming is influenced by the 4 dimensions that make us Who we are—Soul, Heart, Mind, and Body, expressed as Aspiration, Emotions, Thoughts and Sensations—and which determine our Expressions (Inside-Out) and Experiences (Outside-In), i.e., how we perceive and influence our environment, and how we are influenced and perceived by it. Our Being and Behavior shape each other. Everything is connected. Nothing happens in a vacuum. With this 4-dimensional composition, individuals reflect the communities and societies they are part of, which in turn form the countries that ultimately constitute a large part of this Planet. Adopting this twice 4-dimensional perspective translates the ambition to change the world from a naive utopia to a concrete undertaking which starts at the core of the center, with the aspiration of individuals for meaning—a WHY that matters to themselves and others. (Fig. 1)

Each story in Chapter 2 explores the 4 macro-questions that shape an individual's lifelong journey:

WHY are you here? (Purpose, rooted in the Soul/Aspirations), WHO are you? (Personality, related to the Heart/Emotions), WHERE do you stand in life? (Position, linked to the Mind/Thoughts), and WHAT are you doing to align your aspirations and actions (Pro-active stance). Together the answers to these questions illustrate the link between Experience/Sensation and Expression/Action, and the POZE paradigm which they derive from.

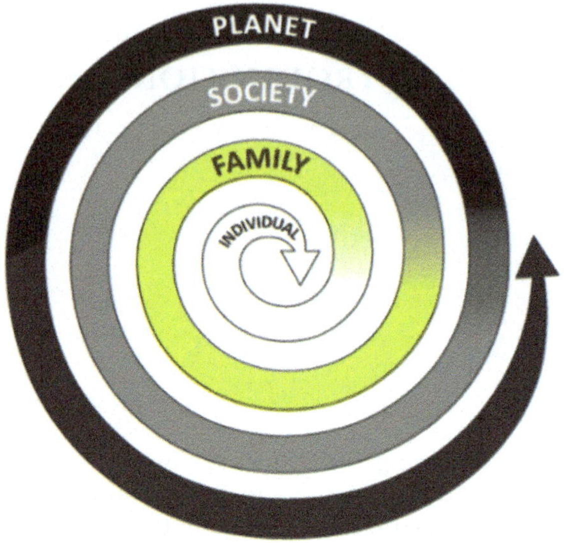

Fig. 1 Spiral Individual to Planet. Everything is connected, from the inside out and from the outside in. The individual is the smallest component of a global system, and part of various communities, which result from biological, social or professional constellations. Individuals and families/communities form society, within the contours of nation states, economies, and cultures. These three dimensions are part of Planet Earth, coexisting with nature. Whatever occurs in one dimension has consequences on the others. Individuals influence the communities they part of, and hereby society, and the planet. Whereas changes in the environment impact the dynamics of society and the communities and individuals that it is made of.

Being Change

The contributions have been selected with a two-folded objective. Firstly, they illustrate that it is possible to align our aspirations and our actions, no matter who and where we are, nor what we have and know. The diversity of location, gender, age, and background illustrates that the link between purpose and passion, desire and deliverable is not as elusive as it sometimes appears whilst we are caught up in our daily routines; they are complementary. There are >8 billion different ways of finding and pursuing meaning in life, and this number is growing with every person who enters this world. Secondly, the aim of this collection is to inspire You, the reader, to begin the path of listening to your inner calling; or, if you are already doing so to encourage you in this endeavor. This book illustrates a small strand of the growing net of likeminded doers and thinkers who have chosen to change and be change for good.

A word of warning—you will be exposed to a brief yet possibly abstract sounding outline of the POZE paradigm in Chapter 1. The aim of this is to offer you the theoretical underpinnings and the overall perspective that the subsequent stories illustrate. The then following tools are meant to help you translate the deriving consequences in your own life. Please remember that words are mere signposts to guide you along the path. They are limited and not meant to be more than transient vehicles. Examine them critically and with an open mind; use the tools to experience whether their content serves You. And ultimately take what is useful for your own journey of transformation.

****

Following a Spiral dynamic, change happens from the inside out, and is nurtured from the outside in. It begins with the aspiration for purpose, and the action that it manifests in. Starting with the intention to find and pursue what matters most to us, our feelings about ourselves and others evolve. This triggers ideas for inner and outer transformation. Gradually our behavior changes, illustrating our intentions. Conversely, every experience activates thoughts, about us, others, and the World. These induce emotions about our own self and our role in society, which influences our journey of being and becoming. Curiosity is a child of mind and heart, which is nurtured by the soul to grow, and manifest in our body through expressions and experiences.

The Spiral is a central theme in nature and science. We are surrounded by reminders of this universal illustration of connection and complementarity. Whether it is the Archimedean spiral that illustrates the POZE paradigm, marked by an even repartition of all rounds which expand from the core to the center, or the Nautilus spiral described by the Fibonacci sequence, illustrating a golden ratio (usually denoted by the Greek letter Phi), spirals are everywhere—in art, in quantum physics, sacred architecture, and in Nature—from sunflowers to ice crystals, from cacti to hair growth, from the DNA double helix over the path of draining water to the galaxies in the universe (Livio, 2003).

To acknowledge, accept and address our inherent desire to find and pursue purpose in a proactive way is the natural instinct of every individual

(Frankl, 1946). Ignoring or subduing this inner impetus is feasible in the short term. In the long term it is counterproductive, to individuals themselves and for the communities they evolve in. Everything is connected. POZE, the paradigm that underpins this book and which will be shortly presented, seeks to help individuals change and be change, in their own context and in Society.

****

BeingChange is structured in 4 chapters. Following an introduction of the intentions and philosophical underpinnings that led to this book (this Introduction), the logic and foundation of the POZE paradigm is briefly explained, as it provides the theoretical framework of this book (Chapter 1). This is followed by a collection of stories from a diverse set of individuals, who look at their own being and becoming through the prism of the POZE paradigm; preceded by the questionnaire that guided their thought process (Chapter 2). I then I use my own journey as an example to show several additional angles through which we can look at our own journey; accompanied by certain lessons learned on the journey to alignment of the dimensions that form who we are; subsequently a collection of tools is introduced to help you explore the nooks and corners of your own past, present and future (Chapter 3).

Life can be looked upon in many different ways: From analyzing the influence of the 4 dimensions of our being and becoming (soul, heart, mind, body), to clusters that marked our journey (people, places, privileges, problems), to answering essential questions (Why, Who, Where, What). From energy arenas (growth, love, work, play) to attitudes. These prisms are complementary. The POZE prism puts them together in a holistic framework which is illustrated by the Spiral that you will encounter throughout this book. We conclude with a summary of patterns that emerge from the presented stories, and the recommendations that derive from this for those who seek to change their own lives, and that of others (Chapter 4).

References

Frankl, V. (1946). *Men's Search for Meaning*. Republication by Paperback (2006).

Livio, M. (2002). *The Story of Phi, the World's Most Astonishing Number*. Broadway Books.

Contents

About the Author

Cornelia C. Walther combines praxis and research. As a humanitarian practitioner, Cornelia worked for nearly two decades with UNICEF and the World Food Program in large scale emergencies in West Africa, Asia and Latin America. As lecturer, coach and researcher, Cornelia collaborates with various universities around the world. Cornelia holds a doctorate in Law and is a certified yoga and meditation teacher. Aside from her interest in the multiple shapes of influence, Cornelia's focus is on social transformation from the inside out, looking at individual aspirations as the point of departure. Her objective is to refine a methodology that influences people towards wanting to get involved in social change processes, rather than obliging them to act for the sake of others. In 2017 she initiated the POZE (Purpose—Optimization—Zenith—Exposure) dynamic in Haiti, offering individuals tools to identify and pursue their aspirations. The network is now expanding into the Americas, Africa, and Europe. Previous publications published by Macmillan Palgrave/Springer include 'Development, Humanitarian Action and Social Welfare'; 'Humanitarian Work, Social Change and Human Behavior'; 'Connection in Times of Covid' and 'Technology, Behavior and Social Change'.

Get in touch with Cornelia via LinkedIn Profile: https://www.linkedin.com/in/corneliawalther.

Website: https://www.poze.cc.

List of Figures

CHAPTER 1

Plant Change from the Inside Out, Nurture It from the Outside In

Abstract This chapter sets the stage with an introduction to the POZE paradigm which is rooted in the connection and complementarity of soul, heart, mind, and body—articulated as aspirations, emotions, thoughts, and sensations (which influence our experiences and expressions). This 4-dimensionality renders each individual a reflection of the 4-dimensional interplay that links individuals, communities, countries, and Planet Earth. The concept of the Scale of Influence is briefly described to outline the subtle yet essential aspects that shape human interactions. The objective herein is to establish a common understanding of the logical and methodological grounding of the causes and consequences of personal and collective change that will be illustrated by the stories in Chapter 2.

Keywords POZE · Paradigm · Connection · Continuum · Complementarity · Awareness · Change

The theoretical foundation of this book is the concept of a "soul-heart-mind-body connection," collected from various conceptual frameworks and traditions, which is used to examine the multi-faceted dimensions of subjective wellbeing and collective progress. We refer to it as POZE.[1] Our attitude and behavior influence the environment we live in; conversely, the context that we shape through our presence and action influences us in

C. C. Walther, *Leadership for Social Change and Development*,
https://doi.org/10.1007/978-3-030-76225-4_1

return. Whereas our perception of the outside influences what happens inside, what happens inside influences how we experience a situation, and accordingly how we (re)act in it. Understanding this ongoing interplay offers pointers to the causes and consequences of the paradigm shift proposed within POZE, and its benefits. Simply put, inner alignment results in better physical and mental health, a kind, pro-social attitude and improved relationships.

We tend to concentrate on that which distinguishes us. And yet, Humans around the world function within the same multi-dimensional kaleidoscope. On the one hand their experiences and expressions are influenced by the same 4 individual dimensions that shape who they are, what they feel, how they think, and what they do. On the other hand they are influencing and influenced by the same 4 collective dimensions via the society they live in. Understanding the principles and the paradigm that underpin our perception of reality, equips us to understand ourselves and others better, which is the condition of genuine influence. Conceived based on this perspective, the *Scale of influence* (Fig. 1.4) offers a framework to assess and shape interpersonal interactions consciously, as a means of influencing human behavior systematically.

POZE is a pragmatic approach to help individuals find and pursue their aspiration for meaning, and thereby consciously influence, and eventually transform their environment. It contributes to individual and collective wellbeing by helping people understand and optimize the interchange between their soul (aspirations), heart (emotions), mind (thoughts), and body (sensations/behavior) proactively; and hereby improve their relations with each other. Based on 20 years of multi-disciplinary research, work and personal experience POZE's modular approach is applicable in any country-context.

What follows is a summary of the foundational principles and concepts that form the POZE Paradigm and the methodology of sustainable social change that derives from it. It is a condensed overview of concepts that have been detailed in several books.[2]

1.1 Dimensions of Humanness

All human beings are a composition of 4 dimensions (soul, heart, mind, and body; expressed as aspirations, emotions, thoughts, and sensations/behavior; furthermore, they evolve in a society that entails 4 dimensions (individuals, communities, countries, planet). Thus, these twice

4-dimensions represent an universal foundation for people to connect as equals.

Every person is part of a collective dynamic. Their personal evolution is influenced by the evolution of the communities and institutions that they belong to, voluntarily or not. Inversely they influence these collective dynamics through their respective being and doing. Intentionally or not, passively and actively, individuals shape their environment and are shaped by it in return. These ongoing streams of influence can be understood, addressed, improved, and gradually optimized.

It is important to understand how the twice 4-dimensional dynamics that determine our individual and social journey influence our being and becoming. Once the multiple layers of connection are acknowledged, they can be analyzed to identify bottlenecks that impede their harmonious flow. Once blocks are recognized, it becomes possible to explore further and find the causes that trigger them. From coping with the consequences of these bottlenecks we then move to understanding where they come from, which is essential to gradually reduce their influence on our emotions, thoughts and actions. Eventually this leads to the optimization of our internal modus operandi, which is conducive to the optimization of the many collective dynamics that we are part of. This optimization is an organic and ongoing process.

Once we understand how we think and feel influences how we experience our environment and express ourselves in it, we can consciously influence these experiences and expressions. It is a continuing journey in which the causes and consequences mutually nurture each other. The ability to consciously influence our own being and behavior, rather than being a bystander of our emotions, instincts and urges, increases our personal wellbeing, and facilitates the interaction with others. It is a process that happens in complementary stages: (1) Once our aspirations, beliefs, feelings, thinking, speech, and behavior are aligned, we experience peace inside, because the "cognitive dissonance" that arises when our values and actions clash, dissolves.[3] (2) Whereas fragmented people subconsciously reproduce their inner fragmentation in their environment, an individual in peace exudes a peaceful authentic presence which is pleasant to others and naturally harmonizes the relationships the individual is involved in; the ensuing positive social atmosphere further contributes to the individual's wellbeing. (3) Deriving from inner wellbeing the desire to connect and share with others in order to contribute to their wellbeing arises naturally; which benefits the communities they evolve in. (4) Living in a harmonious atmosphere is conducive to the mental and physical health of those who initiate the new dynamic, and of those around them; this dynamic grows exponentially the more individuals get drawn in.

What follows is a brief description of the 4 individual dimensions, tailed by an outline of the 4 collective dimensions. This presentation is included here not for the sake of academic interest, but to show the relevance of the manifold connections that shape every human life, and thus help understand the stories in Chapter 2.

1.1.1 Individual Dynamics

- *The Body* is the physical interface between mind and matter, connecting our internal and external realms.[4] It is the channel through which individuals experience their environment and express themselves in it. The body is at the same time conductor and communicator when it comes to the interaction with other people. It is the (double) filter that influences how we perceive others, and how we are perceived by them.
- *The Mind* filters, analyzes and judges the sensorial inputs that enter via the physical membrane. Based on past experiences that were archived as (sub)conscious memories, it draws conclusions and makes decisions that manifest in actions. The thoughts that we entertain result in emotions; thus, the former offer an entry point to get a grip on the latter. Gaining gradual control over the flow of thoughts requires awareness of its causes and consequences.
- *The Heart* keeps us alive, metaphorically and in real terms. Every contraction/expansion of the heart valves is a minuscule part of this intrinsically complicated process that maintains our organism. Similarly, our emotions are the humane, warm, relatable part of our being that makes us social personas who love and loath. Emotions are the current underneath our intellectual deliberations and decision-making processes. It is the trigger that ultimately moves us from deliberation to decision, from aspiration to action.
- *The Soul* is the core of our being. Identifying and fulfilling the purpose of our existence is the start of life. In the process of exploration, we come closer to the best version of ourselves which enables us to share with others who we truly are (Fig. 1.1).

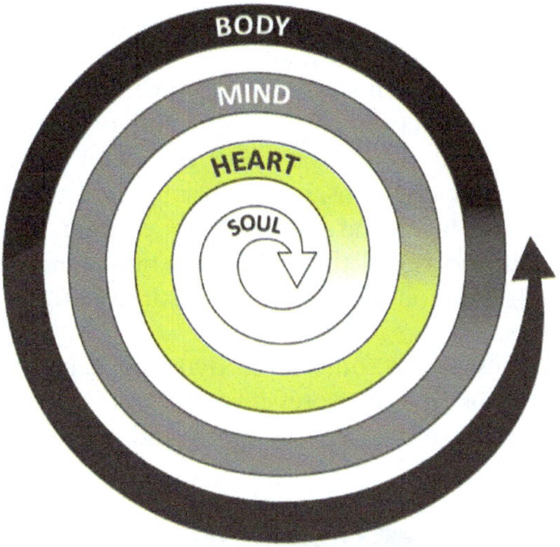

Fig. 1.1 Spiral Soul to Body. Everything is connected, from the inside out and from the outside in. Our soul finds its expression in our aspirations. These influence the heart, which is the source of our emotions. How we feel impacts our mind, thus how we think. How and what we think impacts our behavior. Our experience of "reality" manifests externally in the body which is the interface between our inner and outer space, and it influences what happens inside. On the one hand, we experience physical sensations through our physical sensorial tools, these influence our mind and heart. How we feel and think influences our inner realm, how we perceive our environment and thus how we (re)act in it

The body is a tool to put an anchor in the present. Awareness to physical sensations as experienced via our senses is a step towards awareness of the present in which our thoughts and emotions take place. Such anchoring can serve to take a deliberate distance from emotions that appear overwhelming. While emotions arise and pass beyond our control, gestures and physical sensations can be consciously influenced, which influences the thoughts that derive from the related experience, which impacts the emotions that are triggered by the thought process.

Conversely, awareness to our emotions and thoughts is a way to enhance our physical wellbeing. External events and elements put our inner system under stress. A large part of diseases, from headaches to ulcers to cardiovascular issues, is related to worries, fear, anger that is triggered by our personal or professional environment. Moving away from the automatism of judgement is a gradual process, that is sometimes easier than at other times. It benefits our health, starting with the decrease of blood pressure and reduction of adrenalin and other stress hormones. Once we open our eyes to see the other side, looking at our own life and that of others with the conscious effort to shed the automatic filter of like and dislike, of black and white, colors emerge. When judgement is discarded, differences reveal their beauty. Strict categorizations do not do justice to a world as complex as ours. We surf a rainbow that connects apparent opposites.

This two-way inside-out/outside-in dynamic can be distilled even further when we look at the expression that our 4 dimensions take in the form of aspirations, emotions, thoughts, and sensations (Fig. 1.2).

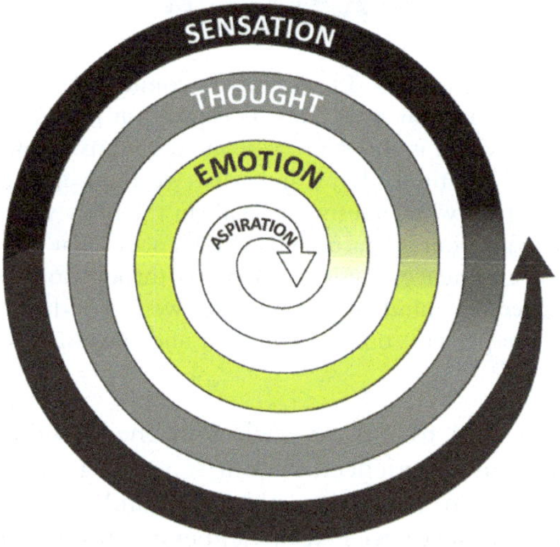

Fig. 1.2 Spiral Aspiration to Sensation. Everything is connected, from the inside out and from the outside in. Our aspirations impact our emotions, which influence our thoughts and hereby our experiences and expressions (sensation). Conversely, the way in which we express ourselves causes certain experiences, which result in physical sensations that trigger thoughts and emotions, which fuel or alter our aspirations; and shape our memories. These memories influence our emotions and thoughts in future situations, and hereby our future expressions and experiences

Aspirations are central to individuals, and individuals are at the center of the continuum that connects people and Planet Earth. Thus, planetary change begins with the personal choice to change ourselves. Like a stone that is dropped into the water triggers expanding waves.

1.1.2 Collective Dynamics

The 4 individual dimensions resemble the 4 collective dimensions that shape Society: Individuals are the smallest entity (micro) of various communities/institutions (meso), together these two constitute countries, economies, cultures (macro). These three dimensions in addition to Nature form Planet Earth (meta).

- *Micro* entails the 4 internal dimensions of the individual (soul, heart, mind, body), and the entirety of the person that is part of a social construct such as an institution or community.
- *Meso* refers to the institutions and communities that are created by and composed of individuals. Every individual is voluntarily or not, knowingly or not, part of various entities; these affiliations may be biological (family), professional (workplace), leisurely (sports-club), or derive from conviction (church, political party). They represent the biospheres that relate to the 4 arenas that human life evolves in (growth, love, work, play)—these will be looked at closer in Chapter 3. These communities represent the interface between the micro and macro dimension.
- *Macro* encompasses micro and meso. It is made of countries and economies. The macro-dimension is a concrete manifestation of human intentions and interactions. It is the (un)desired outcome of systems that were put in place by human beings.
- *Meta* denotes the cumulative of micro, meso, and macro; in addition to non-anthropocentric aspects such as Nature and thus far unexplored features of the world. It also entails supra-national institutions such as the United Nations due to their international mandate.

When we adopt this twice-4-dimensional perspective, the idealistic statement "We can change the World" becomes a pragmatic undertaking that begins at the core of the center with the aspiration of individuals to find meaning and express their best self on Planet Earth (Fig. 1.3).

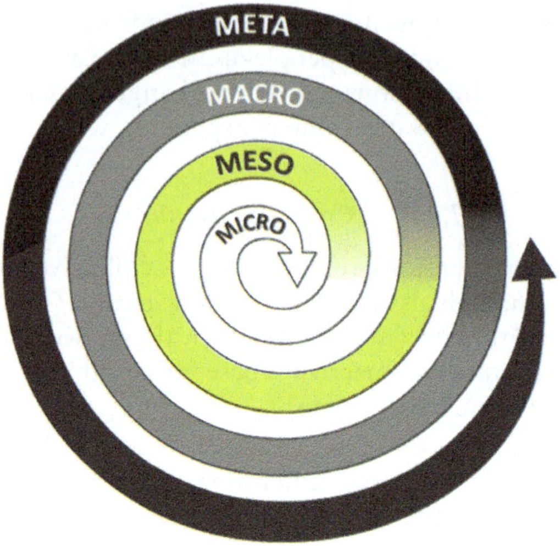

Fig. 1.3 Spiral Micro to Meta. Everything is connected, from the inside out and from the outside in. Individuals represent the micro dimension of a multi-dimensional system. They form, shape, and experience the meso level which results from the communities they are part of (voluntarily or biologically, directly or indirectly). The contours of economic, political, cultural systems form the macro level. Micro, meso, and macro dimensions operate within a meta system that is the interface between the tangible and the immaterial. Within a seamless continuum one dimension is influenced by the others and influences them in return

1.1.3 Universal Principles

To complete the understanding of individual and collective dynamics, it is important to acknowledge 4 principles that apply across all dimensions:

- Change—Everything constantly evolves. Nothing is permanent.
- Connection—Everything is linked to something else which influences it, and which it influences. Nothing occurs in a vacuum.
- Continuum—Everything is part of a larger whole. Isolation is an illusion.
- Complementarity—Everything is part of something else that may be its opposite, and renders it complete. Nothing is perfect by itself.

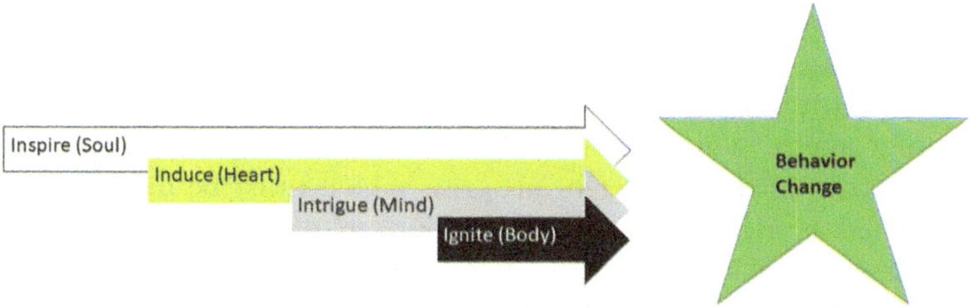

Fig. 1.4 Schema Scale of Influence. The sustainable change of individual behavior involves the 4 dimensions that underpin this behavior: Aspiration (from the awareness that change must happen, to being inspired in one's core to getting involved oneself to make this change happen); Emotions (from automatic reactions to external stimuli to systematically induced emotional responses that are conducive to the cause at stake); Thoughts (from indifference to an informed opinion that is mixed with the curiosity to learn more); and Sensation (from internal deliberations to a shift that manifests the inner change of "mind" into concrete action). The resulting behavior may inspire others to change the way they think, feel and act

1.1.4 Energy Arenas

From the 4 individual dimensions derive the 4 macro-questions that guided the interrogation of those whose stories you will read in the next chapter. They relate to the 4 interrelated energy arenas in which we unfold each dimension, ideally nurturing their interplay: Spiritual development (**Growth**), Relationships (**Love**), Effort (**Work**), and Physical wellbeing (**Play**). Ideally each arena activates all 4 dimensions (soul, heart, mind, body; although it is anchored in one of them) and nurtures the ongoing mutual harmonization within and between the different dimensions and arenas. A short overview is included to close this section since arenas involve both, individual and collective dynamics:

> *Growth*—Spirituality is not limited to religion; it pertains to the personal becoming of an individual's personality. It leads towards the disclosure of their highest self. (It is anchored in or emanating from the Soul.)
>
> *Love*—Relationships may be bilateral or include life in a community. Love for others starts with appreciation of oneself. What has not

been found inside is not to be found outside. (It is anchored in or emanating from the Heart.)

Work—Intellectual and professional pursuit lead to the sense of achievement, which contributes to an individual's sense of satisfaction. It is an outer layer of progress which must be understood and pursued as such. (It is anchored in or emanating from the Mind.)

Play—Sensorial experiences, from pleasure to pain, from safety to sexuality to the satiation of physiological needs, from beauty to bodily enjoyment to material acquisitions and sports, represent the material interface between mind and matter. They tend to consume much time and attention; awareness to this propensity helps to keep them in check. (It is anchored in or emanating from the Body.)

For lasting happiness and fulfillment, an individual must experience and express all 4 dimensions. This may happen in one arena, or across several different ones:

For example, you are on a spiritual path (Growth/Aspiration), spending much of your time in your religious community where you feel connected and welcomed (Love/Emotion). In your free time you seek to learn more about your faith, maybe writing about it (Growth/Thought). You find joy in addressing your "body as a temple" both regarding what goes in, i.e., food, and as to what goes out, i.e., behavior (Play/Sensation). All 4 dimensions are anchored within the arena of *Growth*.

Alternatively, it may require the complementarity of different arenas. Such complementary fulfillment may arise for example, when you are active volunteering against climate change because it is a cause that you care passionately about (Growth/Aspiration); you have a loving partner that supports you and whom you love deeply (Love/Emotion); you have a job that you do not care much about, but it is intellectually stimulating because of the issues you deal with (Work/Thought) and though you do not have much time for exercise you consciously seek to eat a healthy vegetarian diet to protect your body and the planet (Play/Sensation).

Disproportion towards or lack of fulfillment in one dimension and/or in one arena can be (provisionally) compensated, if another one is intensely experienced. Temporarily an imbalance, whereby dimensions are neglected, can thus be coped with. Yet if unevenness lingers it impedes the synchronization of the 4 dimensions, and thus the overall organism. This jeopardizes the mental and physical health of the individual, and their social interactions. Nothing happens in a vacuum—our presence and absence, action and lack thereof influences the environment we evolve in.

1.2 Influence

Influencing someone to adhere to a certain viewpoint (and deriving from it, to adopt a certain type of behavior) involves the body, the mind, the heart, and the soul—of both the influencer and the influenced. Once we increase the influence that we have over our own attitude, and deriving from it on our behavior, we can begin to consciously influence how we are perceived by others; genuine and lasting impact ensues (this dynamic is the underpinning of Influence for Impact, i4i, a concept that will be explained in more detail below). This process is further facilitated by our growing understanding of the intrinsic dynamics that underpin both the appearance/perception and action (the other one's as well as our own).

The *Scale of influence* organizes this logic along a range with 4 actionable stages, from low to high intensity (Fig. 1.4):

1. Inspire the desire to become involved.
2. Induce an emotional re-action regarding the issue at stake.
3. Intrigue interest.
4. Ignite the shift from aspiration to action.

Holistic influence has 4 complementary benefits. Firstly, understanding and addressing our inner workings results in an improved relationship within our own self, which leads to more harmony in our social interactions as we become more serene, optimistic, and pro-active. Secondly, once we understand how we ourselves operate we comprehend better how others operate. From a stance of judgement, we gravitate via understanding to empathy to compassion to changed attitude and action. Thirdly, once we gain influence on our own operating model, we gradually grow the ability to influence others deliberately. Fourth, others perceive us as authentic and thus trustworthy, because our intentions, attitude, words, and behavior are aligned. Altogether the expanding outcome is characterized by improved physical, mental, and social wellbeing; that is spread out due to emotional contagion, and the inspirational effect on others of witnessing prosocial action.

1.3 Transformation

Change starts from the inside out and is nurtured from the outside in.

1.3.1 Individual Change

Change starts from the inside out. Personal purpose is the driver that makes individuals move and stand up. The aspiration for meaning is the core of humanity. It led humankind to explore the unknown and invent new things.

Every individual represents a unique combination of characteristics, skills, resources, and connections. This personal equipment enables every person to accomplish something meaningful, in a unique way. If they do not identify what that is, and/or if they refrain from pursuing the effort that it entails, something precious remains incomplete. Identifying and pursuing a purpose, a mission, is a stepping stone on the way of becoming our own best self. It activates our innate power.

Ultimately the journey of life is about becoming our own best self, and to share this self with others. Once the 4 dimensions of our individual being are synchronized, the natural connection between individual and collective wellbeing emerges. Individuals who manifest their values, not in mere words but through authentic behavior benefit from both, a positive self-image and a positive perception in the eyes of others. Conversely, the ensuing harmonization of their social interactions further nurtures their internal serenity, which strengthens the place which they occupy in their communities.

Change is nurtured from the outside in. Our being and behavior influences our environment and it is influenced by it.

The perception that we have of our WHY (purpose/soul) influences WHO (personality/heart) we are, which influences WHERE (position/mind) we stand in life because it impacts WHAT (pro-active behavior/body) we do individually and as part of a community. The ways in which we manifest our aspirations, in words and actions, influence how others see us. Whereas the experiences that result from our interactions with others influence how we see our Self. Our experiences either nurture a positive vision or they hamper it; either they help or hinder the pursuit of our purpose.

Everything is constantly changing. The past influences the present because our education and social context shape WHO we are (Personality). That Past results from our own expressions and the expressions of others. Archived as memories they influence who we are in the now, and who we aspire to be in the future. WHO we are thus influences how we experience our environment, which impacts how we express ourselves WHERE (Position) we are presently. WHAT we do in situation (Action) influences our experience. This impacts our (sub)conscious memory, which the mind will draw from in the future to assess similar situations.

Memories represent the database that our brain draws on to assess and decide about a (re)action. The challenge is that the mind has evolved to re-act quickly by establishing shortcuts (heuristics) which are prone to errors (bias). Understanding the sub-conscious connection between our mental storage from the past and our urges in a present-day situation enables us to be vigilant. Once we are aware of our tendency to re-act (too) quickly, we can (1) choose to put inner space between the external trigger and our re-action to it; and (2) use the resulting mental buffer zone to choose our action consciously, based on our best knowledge at the time of action, in line with our overall aspirations; rather than re-acting blindly to an external trigger.

1.3.1.1 The Cube of Change

Due to the universal principle of connection (see Sect. 1.1) we can seize any of the four inner dimensions to begin a new cycle of living, consciously influencing purpose-driven (present) interactions that generate positive memories (past) and perspectives (future). The dynamic of change can be initiated from the inside out (Aspiration > Emotion > Thought > Expression/Experience) and from the outside in (Expression/Experience > Thought > Emotion > Aspiration) (see Fig. 1.2). These are some examples:

Purpose–Passion–Positioning–Power

The Aspiration of **purpose** (a WHY) leads to **passion** for a cause or task; this allows us to **position** our objectives strategically whilst aligning our day-to-day energy investment (physical or mental effort) with these objectives. A shift occurs as we move from being the victim of our own semi-automatic processes and a playball of others, towards deliberate behavior that is aligned with our own wishes. Genuine personal em**power**ment ensues.

Compassion–Connection–Coherence–Change
The Emotion of **compassion** enables us to establish genuine **connections** with ourselves and with others. Compassion is conditioned by a non-judgmental attitude which derives from acknowledgement and acceptance of that which is. Once we accept and appreciate our Self our external appearance becomes **coherent** and authentic. The need to hide behind an image dissolve. Energy which had been previously dedicated to pretending is freed up for proactive **change** processes.

Honesty–Honor–Focus–Humility
Thinking with **honesty** about the past, present, and future is necessary to assess the status quo. Once that is done, realistic conclusions can be drawn; which is a shift from wishful thinking to candid deliberation. It conditions our ability to **honor** who we are (not). Based on such objectified assessments we can re-direct the **focus** of our intentions on arenas that require transformation, internally and outside. Acknowledging and accepting WHO we are (not) enables us to address others in a space of **humility** in which everyone has equal value. This influences the position which we occupy in life (WHERE we stand).

Influence–Inspiration–Insight–Impact
Understanding the 4 dimensions that underpin our experiences and expressions enables us to not only comprehend our own operating model but to **influence** it systematically, in view of gradual optimization. Such conscious improvement is an ongoing process. Along the journey it manifests in the growing coherence of our values, words, and actions (WHAT). The resulting authentic appearance is prone to **inspire** others. When we act in a way that reflects our aspiration for meaning, and our awareness to the interplay of the 4 dimensions that underpin everything, we gradually gain further **insights** in our own operating model, and in that of others. Deriving from the resulting combination of influence over the 4 dimensions, and insight into oneself and others, our influence on others gains **impact**.

Table 1.1 The Cube of Change

Change within one dimension	*Change from the inside out and vice versa*			
	Soul	*Heart*	*Mind*	*Body*
Soul	Purpose	Compassion	Honesty	Influence
Heart	Passion	Connection	Honor	Inspiration
Mind	Positioning	Coherence	Focus	Insight
Body	Power	Change	Humility	Impact

Note Change dynamics can start and expand horizontally, vertically, and diagonally. They may operate from the inside out (aspiration > emotion > thought > experience/expression), from the outside in (experience/expression > thought > emotion > aspiration), and fuel transformation within a dimension. An evolution that begins in one dimension organically influences the others

These different pathways can be summarized in the *Cube of Change* which looks at the inner impetus (soul/aspiration), its internal appearance (heart/emotion), its external manifestation (mind/attitude), and its external consequences (body/expression) (see Table 1.1).

The ripple effect of social change starts inside. Internal transformation leads to external change, and conversely, within an ongoing continuum of transformation.

Summarized in concentric squares, the interplay of change processes appears. Though the present illustration is limited by the two-dimensional representation on a page, it offers a glimpse of the ongoing interaction between expressions and experiences. Following the connected course within one dimension the benefit of each, and among all, appears. (i.e., along the outer square: Influence on ourselves results in increased Inspiration by life through living. Permeated by harmony within and without we access ever further insights in our own Self, which Impacts our ability to change ourselves, and the environment we are in.) (Fig. 1.5).

****

Many roads lead to Rome, multiple paths lead towards our Self.

The two following images illustrate the path of aspiration (purpose) [Fig. 1.6] and the path of action (personal power) [Fig. 1.7]. Captions summarize only the two immediate effects without going into each complete vertical sequence which were outlined above, nor the diagonal implications.

Two alternative and complementary paths are open; the path of feeling (compassion) and that of deliberation (positioning):

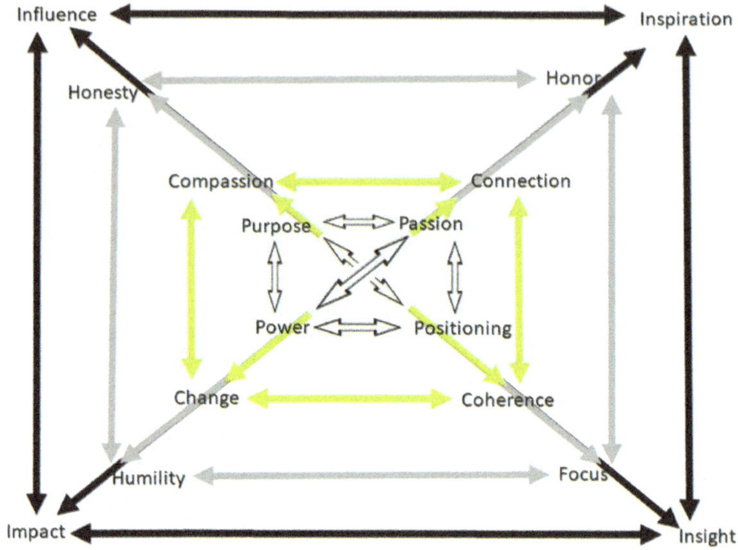

Fig. 1.5 Cubic connections. Expressions and experiences, values and their manifestation influence each other, which has ripple effects within one dimension and among dimensions

The path of feeling—**Passion** (Soul) for a cause takes us to another space of perception. Barriers become stepping stones as our desire to accomplish our mission opens the scope of options. **Connection** (Heart) with others arises in the process, in particular those who share a similar pursuit. As we are moving away from our own interests and worries about our image, we come to **Honor** our beliefs and values, establishing the connection between Mind and Heart. The deriving authenticity that marks our attitude and action is prone to **Inspiration** in others (Body) (see top right corner of Fig. 1.7).

The path of deliberation—Once we have identified what matters most to us, WHY we are here, the sub-conscious **Positioning** (Soul) of our purpose begins. Serving as an inner anchor it gradually leads to emotional **Coherence** (Heart). No longer we are ruled by short-lived desires. The **Focus** (Mind) is set and gradually whatever we say and do is aligned with that aspiration. Analyzing the deriving experiences with the 360-degree understanding of the twice 4-dimensions leads to practical **Insights**

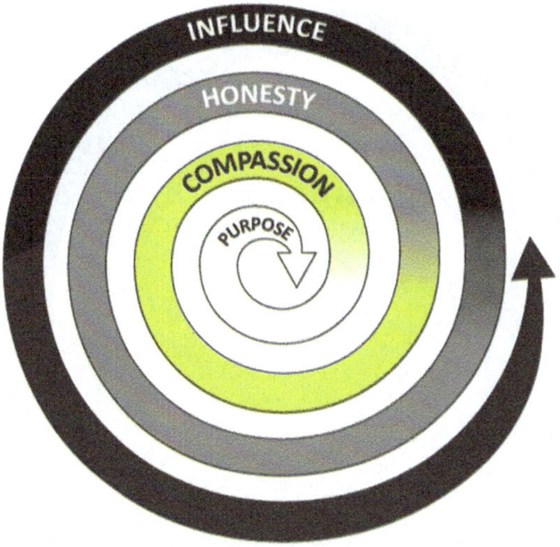

Fig. 1.6 Spiral Purpose to Influence. Everything is connected, from the inside out and from the outside in (starting at the top row of the Cube of Change, from left to right) Purpose instills Passion for a cause and compassion for us and others which nurture each other. Compassion for ourselves builds compassion with others, and hereby Connection, inside and externally. Honestly accepting who we are (not) enables us to Honor us and others without pretention. Our influence on others is conditioned by our ability to consciously influence our own behavior. Conversely, when our action is an honest expression of our values, thoughts, and emotions, we serve our purpose, and hereby Inspire others

(Body) that help us further along the path of purpose (see bottom right corner of Fig. 1.7).

The *Cube of Change* is a magic cube of sorts; dynamics can be triggered in all directions. Taking the perspective of an evolving constantly changing continuum in which everything is connected and complementary expands our internal assessment framework. As nothing happens in a vacuum everything matters, but nothing unfolds by itself. Within that constantly shifting kaleidoscope, nothing is fully separated, and everything stands in complementarity to something else, influencing it while being influenced in return.

****

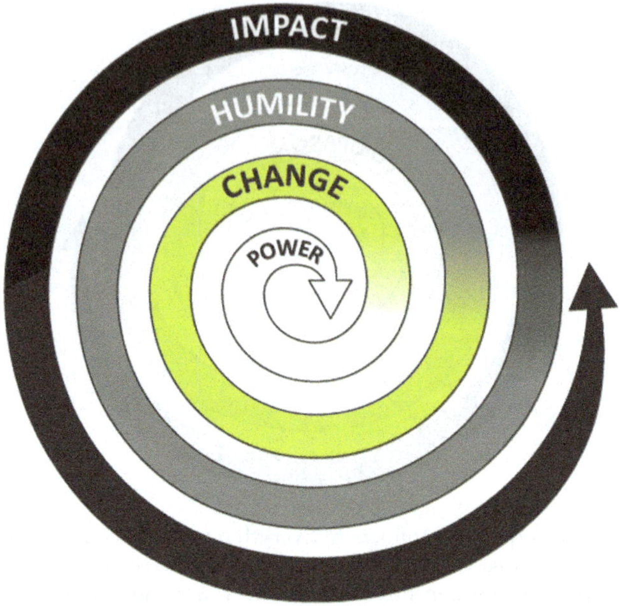

Fig. 1.7 Spiral Personal Power to Social Impact. Everything is connected, from the outside in and from the inside out (starting at the bottom row of the Cube of Change from right to left) As we assess and address our being and becoming consciously we gain ever further Insight in our modus operandi and in that of others. This equips us with the Power to Change ourselves which influences our situation, because we begin to Position our needs and vision with a holistic understanding of the status quo. The Humility that results from such genuine introspection offers Focus and sets the ground for interpersonal Coherence (and thus real Connection); which is essential for sustainable influence on others. Social Change that matters becomes possible. Impact that lasts transforms ourselves and others

1.3.1.2 The Continuum of Being and Becoming One Self

The universal principles of change, connection, continuum and complementarity (Sect. 1.1) apply equally to space as time, to our Self and others. Nothing is ever engraved in stone.

Beyond the looping that operates in the ongoing situation, two other influences operate simultaneously. One that is anchored in the past, and one that is turned towards the future. Whatever experiences occur in the present are influenced by our past, deriving from it. Whatever expressions occur in the present influence our future. This forward-looking influence happens directly, because of the impact that our action has outside, and indirectly, because any experience, physical, mental, and emotional, leaves an imprint on us, and is stored. Via our body, mind, and heart we draw from storage as a (sub)conscious reference point when a new situation arises.

Our Self is a combination of different components. These components continue to evolve with each new experience, and thus do we:

The first component is what we commonly referred to as I/me/mine. It is in itself a composition of 4 dimensions which stand in a constant interplay, influencing each other mutually—soul, heart, mind, and body. It lives in the *present*. This **"Experiencing I"** exists only in the Now. Once the moment is gone, it is gone. Only in the present the soul, heart, mind, and body can take in experiences and manifest in expressions that influence these experiences.

The second component is the **"Evolving I,"** which is an imprint of our *past* aspirations, emotions, thoughts, and sensations. It is a leftover from past expressions of our soul, heart, mind, and body. Anchored in the past, it influences the present, and hereby the future. Whatever impressions we have accumulated from our past experiences and past expressions, influences thus how we perceive our present-day experience, and hereby our expressions in it; thus, it influences our future.

The third component is the **"Being I"** which entails everything that we are, have been, and will be. It is the cause of our *future*.

The fourth component is the **"Meta Self,"** the universal dimension of our being, that is shared by all beings, connecting us in the same realm. It is at the same time part of all other components and constitutes their essence; representing who we have been, are and will be, individually and together. The expressions of the soul, heart, mind, and body are passing phenomena, like ripples on the water; arising and passing, without consequence; unless we pay attention to them. Like stuff that washes ashore at the beach accumulates as time goes by, so the imprints of past expressions pile up in the *Evolving I*. The more attached we are to them the bigger the pile grows. Whatever we concentrate on grows. If our attitude is equanimous, then the *Evolving I* has no additional material to add to the pile, and whatever had already accumulated is gradually washed away. This may sound theoretical. Yet, distilling complex matters such as our being into smaller components can serve to distinguish entry points for change.

Often personal transformation feels like a task that is too big to undertake; looming large it is intimidating. The objective of the multi-dimensional POZE prism, and of the layered presentation in the present pages is to offer you a variety of entry points to choose one that feels sufficiently inviting for you, to take further steps in the direction of disentanglement. Any entry point, any loose end can serve to begin. Because everything is connected.

The Experiencing I is the imprint of where I went, and an indication of where I go. Our (past and present) experiences and expressions shape the *Evolving I* which influences our (present and future) expressions, and hereby our experiences. Being neither good nor bad the Self is always different.

1.3.2 Collective Transformation

1.3.2.1 Being and Becoming Change, Together

Aspirations are the core of our individual existence. They influence who we are and become. We are geared towards the gradual revelation of ourselves in its purest form. Our experiences and expressions refine over time our "self in waiting." Similarly, to a newborn whose immune system is strengthened by the process of birth, the pain of life polishes our personality. Guides, coaches, and teachers are like midwives; their role is not to create but to facilitate the birth of something that exists already.

The constellation of Society—which derives from the meso, macro, and meta dimensions that the individual (micro) is part of—can be purposefully and *systematically* optimized to bring the best possible outcome for each member. The benefit is extrapolated. As the collective seeks to lift everyone towards attaining their higher self it allows the community to fulfill its potential to flourish, by addressing the needs of all those who are part of it.

Individuals are the initiators and the finality of communities, and of Society. What happens in the collective experience is influenced by them and influences them in return. Like individuals who have—whether they are conscious about it or not—the potential to attain their best self, communities and thus society can be deliberately configured and influenced to nurture the best in individuals; which is ultimately in the best interest of the collective.[5] Due to the mutual influence that the 4 individual and the 4 collective dimensions have onto each other every individual benefits when the collective thrives; whereas the collective benefits from the wellbeing of each individual. Briefly said—individual wellbeing is the cause and consequence of collective wellbeing.

1.3.2.2 The Ripple Effect of Conscious Choices

Everything is connected (Fig. 1.8). Our Choices today impact our behavior which has implications for others and the Planet, now and

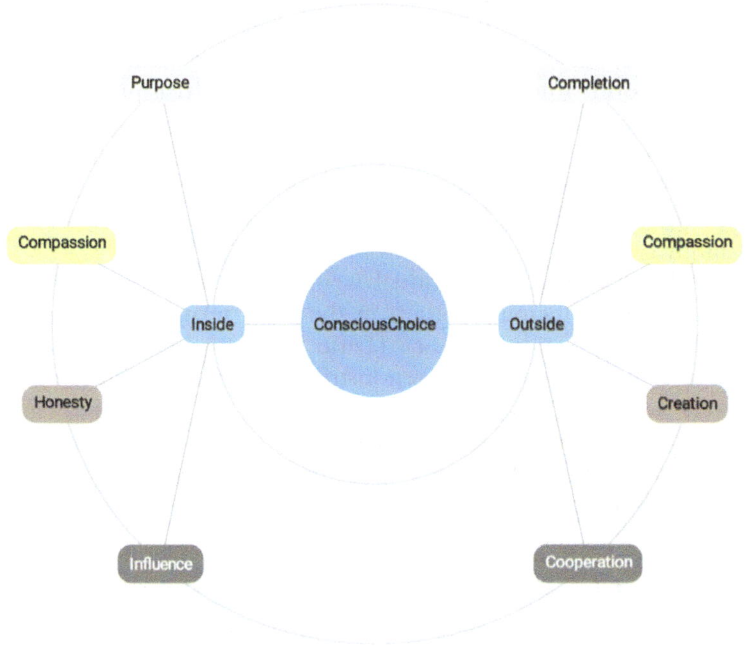

Fig. 1.8 MindMap Conscious Choices. Everything is connected, including the causes and consequences of our choices. Inside—the choices we make derive from our internal reality; they are shaped by our thoughts (mind), emotions (heart), and aspirations (soul). Outside—Conversely, our choices influence our external attitude, appearance, and ultimately our actions (body). Starting to change who we are and what we do, begins thus with the conscious decision to change something, followed by the decision on a course of concrete action, and its pursuit in practice

tomorrow. In 2020 the COVID-19 Pandemic acutely reminded us of the interconnectedness of everything and everyone. We can acknowledge, accept, and address this lesson, or ignore it and continue to tinker with surface symptoms (Walther 2020c).

1.4 Reciprocity

The principle[6] of reciprocity has been recognized and reflected in cultures for centuries. Commonly referred to as "the Golden Rule" it states that we should do to others what we desire for ourselves and refrain from doing to them what we would not want to be done to ourselves. It has found entry in one way or another in religions and belief systems around the world. Interestingly, modern science increasingly proves that this wisdom of the past is not only a natural reflection of something that is part of our "moral blueprint" (Haidt 2006)[7] but that is in our best interest to respect and address the interests of others.[8]

Life begins when we acknowledge that we are not alone and act accordingly.

In the long term, our individual wellbeing depends on actions that we take for the wellbeing of others in the short term. The longstanding paradigm of *homo homini lupus est* (Latin for "man is wolf to man") has served for centuries as an unspoken justification for ego-centric behavior. However, an attitude of *homo homini lux est* (Latin for "man is light to man") is part of our human evolution. Cooperation is enshrined in our DNA; it is the principal reason why humanity has survived and evolved thus far (Nowak 2011).[9]

1.4.1 The Win–Win-Win–Win of Solidarity

What we do for others furthers our own interests as well as theirs. When our inner beliefs and external behavior are aligned, we find internal peace and collective harmony. Individuals who act to further the wellbeing of others benefit in 4 direct and 4 indirect ways[10]:

1.4.1.1 Direct Benefits

Win-1—when they act in line with their personal values, and the inherent aspiration of being "good," they cultivate a positive self-image (soul);

Win-2—the act of helping leads to the emission of endorphins [body]; this hormone is connected to the subjective feeling of happiness (heart);

Win-3—experiencing how the receiver of the benevolent act benefits, enhances the positive experience of the one who has acted because s/he understands the connection between action and impact, or how they have made a difference (mind).

Win-4—As their action enhances the wellbeing of someone else who is part of the same meso and macro environment as themselves, the betterment of the receiving person's situation contributes to an improvement in the overall situation and the prevailing inter-personal atmosphere. In the case of an institution the accumulation of this type of action eventually affects the prevailing organizational culture that the person evolves in, which is beneficial to everyone [body].

1.4.1.2 Indirect Benefits

Win-5—Behaving in a kind, helpful manner influences how the person is perceived by others. When that type of behavior is repeated over time it leads others to trust and appreciate them more.

Win-6—The repetition of a certain behavior strengthens the underpinning synaptic connections. This makes that behavior easier over time. Thus, what was initially a conscious effort turns into a natural action, that still yields the aforementioned benefits.

Win-7—Bystanders who observe the act of kindness not only see their own mood enhanced, they are inspired to echo the pro-social behavior, which may benefit other people in their environment, including the person who took the initial action.

Win-8—The snowball effect of a pay-it-forward dynamic is triggered, which impacts Society positively (and eventually the person who offered the "seed kindness").

It is in everyone's interest to acknowledge and actively address the interests of others, and yet the track from awareness of this fact, to appreciating it as relevant to oneself, to accepting it as a necessity, to actually applying it through one's personal action is not always straightforward. The question is to move from theory to practice, and furthermore from the feeling of obligation to the *desire* of getting involved. This is the purpose of 4 methodologies deriving from the overall paradigm, which are addressed next.

1.4.2 POZE in Action

The challenge is to make people *want* to be part of social solutions.

To this end, POZE addresses social change from different angles. Together they form a circular embrace of the 4 dimensions that determine human existence, which is a combination of experiences and expressions. This is done using 4 methodologies to proactively and systematically generate positive social transformations; the:

- Empowerment of individuals (P4P—Purpose for Power),
- Enhancement of institutional culture in the non-profit sector (C4C—Compassion for Change),
- Enlargement of personal leadership potential (H4H—Honesty for Humility) and
- Expansion of influence to build social good at scale (i4i—Influence for Impact).

Anchored in the POZE logic they contribute to clearly defined, measurable goals: *Purpose for Power* concentrates on the empowerment of the individual, independent of an institution. *Compassion for Change* is for institutions and organizations, as it focuses on individual reconnection as a means towards institutional cultural change. *Influence for Impact* is geared towards the systematic use of individual and collective decision-making processes to shape systemic dynamics. Common to all is *Honesty for Humility*, which is about personal authenticity (or, about individuals becoming their best self), is meant for individuals at all levels, anywhere. It has affinities to what in some contexts is referred to as "leadership".[11]

Each approach is anchored in one particular dimension, yet they operate on the interplay of all 4 dimensions. While distinct in their scope, with differing prime audiences, each approach is anchored in the understanding that individuals have the power to change themselves and their lives, and to make a difference in the lives of others. This is irrespective of age, education or socioeconomic status. The POZE paradigm is rooted in the belief that we can, must, and will be the change we want—if we choose to change WHO (aspiration/purpose) we are and WHAT (action/behavior) we do. A short overview of the 4 methodologies that serve this process:

Purpose for Power (P4P) gives individuals tools to identify and pursue meaning. By helping individuals to identify and connect with their own Purpose it enables individuals to unlock their inherent Power to overcome challenges and thrive despite these challenges. Primary audiences and beneficiaries are aid workers, young people, the elderly, teachers, and social workers. Central entry points are school curricula, parental education programs, retirement residences, and employee well-being programs. It is anchored in the soul.

Compassion for Change (C4C) offers an approach for nonprofit institutions that seek to reignite Compassion and value awareness among their staff. The result is improved staff well-being, motivation, and performance. As staff members begin to live and practice personally the principles and values which they promote in public, the institution's impact in the arenas of their mandate increases, and with it the institutional reputation; the latter further supports the positive impact because the trust of donors and so-called "beneficiaries"[12] increases which is conducive to both the organization's funding (donors) and its programmatic results on the ground. C4C helps build a bridge between staff aspirations and organizational vocation, thus connecting individual and institutional missions. Such harmonization between their staff and their cause is indispensable for nonprofit organizations that thrive on public enthusiasm towards a social cause. It is anchored in the heart.

Honesty for Humility (H4H) brings everything together in a framework of authentic leadership. It offers guidance to accompany the process of unveiling the best version of each individual. Honest introspection is the central pillar from which everything else flows naturally. Therefore, while seeking to be useful along the way, H4H acknowledges that the prime step towards leadership must be taken alone, by the individual who is ready.

Influence for Impact (i4i) systematically uses and addresses human aspirations, emotions, thoughts, and sensations to induce desire and readiness for change among individuals and the wider public. Drawing on the *Scale of Influence* (Sect. 1.2/Fig. 1.4) i4i supports the design of communication and advocacy efforts that assist and guide audiences through the process of understanding a situation to having a personalized feeling about the issue at hand to caring enough about this matter to act and change the status quo. It is anchored in the body, which is the only interface between our internal and external reality. Differently said, i4i applies the POZE logic by *Nudging* people to step out of their comfort zone, while *Numbing* their natural inertia it *Nurtures* new behavior patterns, that gradually become new social *Norms* (a process which could be described as an *NNNN-sequence*).

Looking at the *Cube of Change* (Sect. 1.3.1) it appears that each methodology transitions via an intermediate stage on the way to the target objective. In the light of these methodologies, it is possible to summarize the dynamics of change introduced in section 1.3.1.1 as:

Purpose 4 Power: From Purpose 2 Passion 2 Power
Finding and pursuing our purpose awakens the passion for our mission, which fuels the power to overcome any challenge that might arise.

Compassion 4 Change: From Compassion 2 Connection 2 Change
Allowing compassion for ourselves and others enables us to connect with our inner self, and with those around us, which establishes the foundation of change that matters and lasts.

Influence 4 Impact: From Influence 2 Inspiration 2 Impact
When we acknowledge the different dimensions of our being, we can begin to understand them, which is the precursor of influencing them systematically. When our aspirations and actions are aligned, our behavior inspires others to change themselves, which is needed for sustainable impact.

Honesty 4 Humility: From Honesty 2 Focus 2 Humility
Being honest about who we are (not) dissolves the veil of hypocrisies. It enables us to focus on our own strengths and weaknesses, which leads to the honest humility that underpins genuine human interactions.

****

Summing Up: Key Messages of the POZE Paradigm
Everything is connected. Change at the micro-level (individual) influences what happens at the meso (community), macro (country) and thus meta (world) level.

Interpersonal dynamics can be influenced proactively to constantly improve and gradually optimize the outcomes for everyone and the collective which they are part of.

Individuals' aspiration for meaning is the center of the core of global transformation.

The happiness of others conditions our own wellbeing (Fig. 1.9).

****

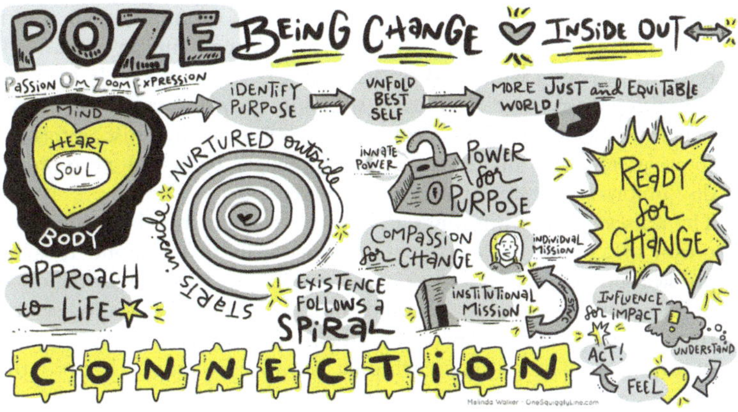

Fig. 1.9 POZE ArtMap. Change starts from the inside out (Aspiration) and is nurtured from the outside in (Action)

NOTES

1. POZE has 4 meanings: it (i) translates as 'inner peace' from Haitian Creole, country where the dynamic was started; (ii) is an acronym that encompasses the 4 core concepts of the paradigm (Purpose, Om, Zoom, Expression); (iii) is a representation of the 4 outcomes of the logic (Perspective, Optimization, Zenith, Exposure); and it (iv) stands for an exercise to nurture inner peace daily (Pause, Observe, Zoom in, Experience), which is a verbal representations of the 4 dimensions that determine human existence (aspirations, emotions, thoughts, and sensations). The POZE methodology encompasses, among other elements, Purpose for Power (P4P), Compassion for Change (C4C), Honesty for Humility (H4H), and influence for impact (i4i). The patterns that emerge from the stories in Chapter 2, relating to Attitude and Mindset, thus connecting the dots of the perspective presented in this book, will be explored in Chapter 4.
2. For details on the concepts and methodologies that are touched briefly upon herein please refer to the referenced books. Walther (2020a) (on the multidisciplinary underpinning of POZE and the deriving methodologies); Walther (2020b) (on the journey of experience and research that led to the paradigm; this book further outlines the impact that it had and can have in organizations dedicated to social change); Walther (2020c), (on a potential way out of the COVID-19 conundrum and the systemic social paradox that it exposed); and Walther (2021) (on technology as a

driver of social change at scale, with a focus on aspirational algorithms and valuable wearables). Each of these books contains an extensive list of references from a wide field of disciplines.

3. Cognitive dissonance refers to a situation involving conflicting attitudes, beliefs, or behaviors. This produces a feeling of mental discomfort leading to an alteration in one of the attitudes, beliefs, or behaviors to reduce the discomfort and restore balance (Festinger 1957).
4. The senses connect our inner and outer environments. Following the definition of a sense as 'a group of sensory cells that respond to a specific physical phenomenon, and that corresponds to a particular region of the brain where signals are received and interpreted', neurologists expand the traditional five senses (sight, smell, taste, touch, audition) to at least nine senses. Besides the traditional set they include: Thermoception—the sense of heat (there is some debate that the sense of cold may be a separate sense); Nociception—the perception of pain; Equilibrioception—the perception of balance; and Proprioception—the perception of body awareness (Close your eyes and touch your nose, if you managed to do so, your sense of proprioception works). Eco-psychologists put the number of available senses at 53 (Cohen 1994). Their definition of a sense goes beyond the physiological phenomenon/nerve sensor definition—the resulting list can be broken down in 4 categories: radiation senses (e.g., sense of color, sense of moods associated with color, sense of temperature); feeling senses (e.g., sensitivity to gravity, air and wind pressure, and motion); chemical senses (e.g., hormonal, such as pheromones, sense, hunger, thirst); and mental senses (pain, external and internal, mental or spiritual distress, sense of self, including friendship, companionship and power, psychic capacity).
5. The universe is an organically evolving kaleidoscope, which illustrates the 4 principles that underpin the POZE paradigm—Change, Connection, Continuum and Complementarity. There is neither good nor bad just different in that evolution, as time and space are relative. With that understanding it becomes natural to engage within the ongoing quest for an optimization of the status quo. This quest in itself illustrates the interconnectedness of everything—because as our own life and living evolves, progressing or regressing, it influences and is influenced by the Universe that it is part of (see also Bohme 1980). There is no guarantee of such optimization (Gould 1996); however our Why is geared towards its pursuit.
6. As this perspective represents a radical shift for many who have grown up with the firm belief that self-interest is the prime motivator of humans, and that this is necessary for survival, this section includes some external references for additional reading for readers.

7. Anchored in the soul are our values—the cornerstone of our belief systems, which in turn underpin our short-term desires and longer-term aspirations. Cross-cultural studies have shown that five human values come from a common pool innate in human nature: harm/care, fairness/reciprocity, in-group/loyalty, authority/respect, and purity/sanctity (Haidt 2006).
8. Humans are hardwired to cooperate, and whatever one does for others has benefits in both directions, for the one who acts and the one who's acted for. Moreover, benefits of pro-social action occur on four levels. The very act of giving back to the community boosts a person's happiness, health, and sense of physical well-being (Plante 2012). Beyond benefit for the one who acts and the one who is acted for, others who witness altruistic acts experience renewed hope, appeasement, and the desire to take similar action (Ramey 2016). From such an expanding attitude of kindness and care among individuals, society overall benefits as the occurrence and acceptability of inequality and deprivation shrink (Pickett and Wilkinson 2009).
9. Cooperation may appear to go against our ingrained instinct of purveying first to our own needs. However, supporting others in an effort of sharing is part of our DNA. It is the reason why humankind has reached the present stage of evolution (Nowak 2011).
10. For a detailed outline of the win–win-win–win effect and its scientific underpinnings, please see (Walther 2020a, c). Some Interesting background readings include the following: on the link between emotion, thought, and action (Lehrer 2010), on our (ir)rational thought process (Kahneman 2007), regarding the connection between behavior and brain structure (Doidge 2007); and on the impact that short and long-term behavior changes have on society (Bicchieri 2017).
11. **'Leadership'** is one of those terms that has been (over) used. Though it usually comes with a positive connotation—it is rarely precisely circumscribed. In the context of H4H and within the present book, Leadership refers to the ability of helping individuals help themselves, to reveal the best version of themselves. This is independent of formal power, and begins with the personal manifestation of the 4 core assets: Purpose-orientation, Compassion for oneself and others, Honesty towards oneself and others, and Influence on our own Self based on conscious attention to the dimensions that constitute it. "Guide" might be a better word than "leader"; because we can only give pointers regarding a path that we have walked ourselves. Another alternative wording is 'agent of change', because one can indicate the path to the bridge, but not carry the passenger over the river. Genuine leaders are those who are able to change themselves, and in doing so affect others to change themselves. It is anchored in the mind.

12. **'Beneficiary'** is another (over) used term, especially in the jargon of Aid. It often comes with a negative connotation. The person labeled as a 'beneficiary' appears as the passive recipient of a well-intended transaction. This terminology is misleading as genuine help is not a unilateral act. To matter and last aid must be provided within a relationship of mutual respect. Partner might be a better word than beneficiary.

References

Bicchieri, C. (2017). *Norms in the Wild: How to Diagnose, Measure, and Change Social Norms*. New York, NY: Oxford University Press.

Bohme, D. (1980). *Wholeness and the Implicate Order*. Routledge & Kegans Paul.

Cohen, M. (1994). Counseling and Nature: A Greening of Psychotherapy. Retrieved (Nov 2020). https://files.eric.ed.gov/fulltext/ED374387.pdf.

Doidge, N. (2007). *The Brain That Changes Itself: Stories of Personal Triumph from the Frontiers of Brain Science*. New York, NY: Viking Press.

Festinger, L. (1957). *A Theory of Cognitive Dissonance*. California: Stanford University Press.

Gould, S. J. (1996). *Full House: The Spread of Excellence from Plato to Darwin*. New York: Harmony Books.

Haidt, J. (2006). The Moral Roots of Liberals and Conservatives. TED. Retrieved (Aug 2020) https://rb.gy/fep1gt.

Kahneman, D. (2007). *Thinking Fast and Slow*. New York: Palgrave Macmillan.

Lehrer, J. (2010). *How We Decide*. Boston: Mariner Books: Houghton Mifflin Harcourt.

Nowak, M. (2011). *SuperCooperators: Altruism, Evolution, and Why We Need Each Other to Succeed, with Roger Highfield*. New York: Martin Free Press.

Pickett, K., Wilkinson, R.G. (2009). *The Spirit Level: Why More Equal Societies Almost Always Do Better*. London: Allen Lane.

Plante, T. G. (2012). Helping Others Offers Surprising Benefits. *Psychology Today*. Retrieved (July 2021) https://www.psychologytoday.com/us/blog/do-the-right-thing/201207/helping-others-offers-surprising-benefits-0.

Ramey, S. (2016). The Benefits of Witnessing Acts of Kindness. Retrieved (July 2021) https://exploringyourmind.com/benefits-witnessing-acts-kindness/.

Walther, C. (2020a). *Development, Humanitarian Aid and Social Welfare: Social Change from the Inside Out*. New York: Palgrave Macmillan.

Walther, C. (2020b). *Humanitarian Work, Social Change and Human Behavior: Compassion for Change*. New York: Palgrave Macmillan.

Walther, C. (2020c). *Connection in the Times of COVID: Coronas Call for Conscious Choices*. New York: Palgrave Macmillan.

Walther, C. (2021). *Technology, Social Change and Human Behavior: Influence for Impact*. New York: Palgrave Macmillan.

CHAPTER 2

Living Change Out Loud

Abstract The present voices of social practitioners, academics, and artists, in both the public and private sectors, illustrate the POZE paradigm. Like each of us, the selected individuals influence in one capacity or another the lives of those in their direct and wider environment. As many of them occupy a leadership position, this influence is multiplied. In this collection, particular attention is given to the breaks and transitions that led the featured people from average to extraordinary, from comfort to compassion, from purpose to personal power. The selection includes formal leaders, as well as individuals who remain under the radar yet mark those who live in their vicinity by their behavior and presence. The aim herein is to make the reader understand and feel that contributing to social change is not an abstract concept but a tangible, feasible, and beneficial dynamic, that is at everybody's reach. What is presented here seeks to (1) illustrate the universal applicability of a twice 4-dimensional perspective and the implications that derive from it; (2) offer common and unusual insights in social dynamics, through the eyes of those who help change them; (3) ignite in readers (You) the desire to get started on the path of purpose; and (4) show examples to get started.

Keywords Testimonial · Optimization · Honesty · Humility · Influence · Acceptance · Values

C. C. Walther, *Leadership for Social Change and Development*,
https://doi.org/10.1007/978-3-030-76225-4_2

The following testimonials are structured around the above-mentioned dimensions of the POZE paradigm (Chapter 1)—Soul, Heart, Mind, and Body, which find their expression as Aspirations, Emotions, Thoughts and Sensations. These 4 dimensions correspond to the 4 arenas in which we invest our energy: Spiritual evolution (Growth), Relationships (Love), Learning and effort (Work), and Material satisfaction (Play).

Finding and revealing our best self is not about adding more layers, but about removing the existing ones; to uncover what is waiting underneath. A questionnaire based on the Honesty for Humility (H4H) methodology (Sect. 1.4.1) offers entry points to begin this journey. The questions are designed to help the explorer dig into the 4 macro-questions (Why, Who, Where, What) that derive from the 4 interrelated dimensions of the POZE paradigm. Asking and answering them offers us personal purpose pointers:

1. *WHY are you here?* It derives from the Soul's quest for meaning;
2. *WHO are you?* It connects to the person inside, the Heart that is alive underneath social layers such as title, status, possessions, relationships.
3. *WHERE are you?* It assesses the current position in life; and the vision that a person has in Mind of their desired environment.
4. *WHAT are you doing to align your aspirations and actions?* It activates the potential of transformation in the Body. Linking the present-day situation to the Self that one aspires to be considers the past without judgement; as a simple point of departure.

As you are reading through the stories you may notice that the 4th macro-question asked and answered is different from the one in the Questionnaire. Rather than "WHAT are you doing to align your aspirations, emotions, thoughts, and actions"? they were asked "WHAT would you like to change, to align your aspirations, emotions, thoughts, and actions"? (Other than testing your vigilance in reading) the reason for this difference is that the selected journeys already illustrate an ongoing dynamic of alignment. The amended question is thus aimed to find out what (more) can be done (Fig. 2.1).

To explore each macro-question each participant/explorer/contributor in this chapter was asked the following ten questions:

Fig. 2.1 Spiral Why to What. Everything is connected. The 4 basic questions that underpin our existence are as interwoven, and the deriving answers are as unique as the individual who answers them. Contemplating with an open mind how these questions relate to our own situation, including our role in Society is useful, and has practical implications. Because acknowledging and accepting the status quo, is the only way forward, towards changing something. Identifying Why we are here; Who we are right now; Where we stand; and What our contribution is, is the only path to the future we want

1. *How would you summarize your life's journey until now?*
2. *Which were the watershed moments of Your Story?*
3. *Are your choices mostly influenced by aspirations, by emotions, by rationality or by material considerations? Has this weighting shifted over time?*
4. *When did an experience completely change your beliefs?*
5. *WHY do you aspire to live (What is your Purpose)?*
6. *WHO do you feel you are as a human being? (How would you define yourself without a name or job?)*
7. *WHERE do you think you are in your life? WHERE do you think you will be when it ends?*

8. *WHAT would you like to change to fully align your aspirations, emotions, thoughts, and action?*
9. *How would you rate the following 4 life-philosophies on a scale [1 (most important)–4 (least)]?*

   - *Purpose for Power (Aspiration)*
   - *Compassion for Change (Emotion)*
   - *Honesty for Humility (Thought)*
   - *Influence for Impact (Behavior)*

   Why did you choose this rating?
10. Is there an advice that you would give to your younger self?

A word of explanation on Question 9—The contributors were asked to rate the relevance of the 4 methodologies that are part of the POZE concept in their own life (Sect. 1.4.2). Their answers derive** from the natural association that comes when reading the word constellations, and the dimensions and values that underpin them. It should be noted that the patterns that seem to emerge from the rankings (Annex B) are yet to be statistically corroborated. Whereas the sample of contributions included in this collection is small due to the page limitations of the present book, the group of like-minded individuals is much larger and keeps on expanding.

The present questionnaire served as a roadmap for the stories, thus allowing patterns to emerge. Yet, flexibility was given to each individual to carve out the uniqueness of their story. The aim herein is to show on the one hand the broad diversity of expressions that purpose-orientation can take, and on the other hand to distill the key parameters that are at play during the transition that leads an individual from being an observer to becoming an actor, from being a victim to being a champion in their own life and that others.

The stories in this chapter were selected to help You look at your own story differently, to discover the beauty underneath. Joining those whom you discover here I am sharing a glimpse of my own story in the next chapter.

2.1 PEOPLE[I]

A list of all contributors is available at the end (Annex A).

Destination Unknown

Lee Kim, Global Congress Lead, Pfizer Innovative Health & Innovation, USA
Born in Jejudo, South Korea

Lee is a designer thinker, an engineer, a poet (when she is in pain), and a community builder. Outside her 9–5 job, she founded a community innovation lab—Design Dream Lab where anyone with a giving heart can create an impact and dream of a better future. In 2020, she built three additional virtual communities—Design Thinking Zeal, H.U.G. (Humans in Unbelievable Gatherings), and Enchanted Playground—all aiming to bring more human connection to the world that is so isolating. Lee loves building and fostering creativity through everyday experiences and finds joy in connecting dots with other fun-loving and joyful human beings. She also loves to make stuff (up)!
Life as Parts Making a Whole

I have constructed my life in six parts:

Part 1: In Awe of Outside World

Growing up in a small island, the closest to modern technology we experienced was seeing the buses that came through our village a few times a day. The world outside the island became visible when we got a TV when I was in 3rd grade. I was in awe of the world outside the island—the cities with tall buildings, lights that were beaming from every window… that world looked brighter than moon light that shone over the unpaved road in our village. I left the island when I was 11 to go to boarding school in Seoul.

Part 2: Fear of Failure

It became clear to me in high school that I would not be able to get into a good college which promised to be the pathway to a successful life. I saw myself as a failure—a concept that I couldn't quite accept. I convinced my parents to send me to America.

Part 3: Doing What Is Expected

In college, I pursued an Engineering major purely based on my need to get a job and a working visa after my graduation.

Part 4: Seeking What Brings Me Joy

Only after getting steady paychecks and getting my work visa, the thought of pursuing something more joyful entered my mind. For some reason, quilting became an obsession during this time—joining quilting bees, purchasing fabrics…sewing all the time! Eventually that led me to enroll in Fashion Institute of Technology and I got a degree in Fashion Design. This experience was truly magical. Creating something that wasn't there. Making your own design come alive with fabrics. However, I didn't pursue fashion design as my life's path. I realized creativity alone wasn't enough for me to give up my steady job.

Part 5: Losing My Family and Finding My Way

7 years ago, I had a huge fight with my parents when I visited them with my new-born baby. They disowned me and I left South Korea with a heavy heart. A few months later, I was introduced to Design Thinking and also met my mentor, friend, Tracy who truly cared about the work she was doing and gave me a way to apply empathy to reconnect with my parents. Human-centered Design thinking mindset allowed me to look beyond the obvious. With this new found perspective in life, I was able to reconcile with my parents.

This time, I was convinced that creativity + empathy + mindset of design thinking would allow me to explore what brings meaning in my life. I left my engineering career and joined Pfizer to bring design thinking to the team I joined—Global Congress Center of Excellence.

At the same time, the idea of Design Dream Lab was born. This collective was created to bring empathy-driven design thinking to the community we live in. We wanted to build a place where the members of the community can co-create solutions regardless of their proficiency in design or design thinking process.

Part 6: Finding Our Way Through Crisis

Last year, when Covid-19 forced us to be in isolation, the world became very dark for me (internally). I didn't know how to truly have "meaningful" conversations, build connections, facilitate workshops, and co-create solutions virtually.

This was when I reached out to many of my partners in life to build virtual communities.

Four different communities were built in 2020 and one more is being born this year.

1. Design Thinking Zeal—It is a global community of design thinkers. My co-curator brings strategic mind, virtual facilitation skills, and intentionality of building a truly diverse community.
2. H.U.G. (Humans in Unbelievable Gatherings)—It is a global community of conveners. My partner brings great knowledge and experience in the event industry as well as an open, curious and humble approach to designing each gathering.
3. Enchanted Playground—It is a community built to use "play" as a way to engage with one another. Co-maintenance person of this playground is all about play, improve, and brings such positive energy to the playground.
4. Design Dream Lab virtual Café—It is a global community where we apply empathy to look at the world and solve problems. Co-curator of this community cares deeply about holding space for each other and is always available for ideation, facilitation, and for support.
5. Identity Lab—Gallery of Us (will be born this year)—This community will be about experimentation and exploration. My laboratory partner is an explorer, strategic thinker, and a doer.

These communities were built so that we can collectively find ways to bring more meaningful connections though constant experimentation!

My life truly began when everything fell apart

Part 5: When my parents disowned me, the world became very dark for me. But I still thought I was right. Logic dictated my reasoning and I didn't know how to apply empathy. So when empathy-based human-centered design was presented to me, this changed everything. The realization that there is no such thing as "absolute truth" hit me hard. The idea forced me to be more curious, and approach the world with more humility. What would it like to be my mother before she was my mother… ? That type of questioning changed the way I view the world.

Meeting Tracy who showed me the power of empathy was the moment that shifting happened. However, without losing my parents and going through the pain, I am not certain if I would have felt the power of empathy as much as it did.

Life is a journey with constant exploration influenced by many things
Part 1: This was influenced by aspiration. Wanting to see the outside world! Be part of the world out there! The island seemed too small.
Part 2: This was influenced by social pressure of "success." The options presented were not applicable to me.
Part 3: This part was influenced by material consideration. The focus was to get a job at a reputable company which would sponsor me for my working visa and reasonable pay.
Part 4: this part was influenced by "emotions": What brings me energy and joy. Exploring the answers to those were my focus.
Part 5: This part was first influenced by rationality when I was fighting my parents about what is right and what is wrong. Then when I found my way via Design thinking mindset, it was influenced by different perspective taking which I can say probably have more to do with Emotion with rationality. I am also profoundly grateful for the opportunities that were given to me by Tracy. I wonder if I didn't meet her, if she didn't give me the opportunities, if I didn't get the chance to see the impact that we were creating, what would I be doing today?
Part 6: This part was influenced by aspiration. What we can create together is so much greater than what I can create alone. The world needs us. And we need each other. By creating these communities, I believe we can bring collective impact that can also transform individual lives.

Reframe
When I realized that my parents and I were looking at the world through different frames, the world changed for me. Being able to reframe the world through different perspectives allowed me to seek different questions rather than forcing my answers.

There is a reason for our existence
Because we all can be a tiny light to those who are seeking the pathway. Tracy with Design Thinking mindset and empathy-driven problem solving was that for me. My purpose now is to find as many partners in the world who may not have discovered their own power, and co-create something together that eventually makes a world with more purpose driven change makers. It is so much better when you know that you don't have to take on the journey alone.

Being human
Explorer. Currently, I am exploring ways to create meaningful experience so that each of us can discover continuously what makes our heart filled with joy, wonder, and awe.

Taking a pause. Reflecting
Currently, I am at the teenage stage… I may know enough to read, to make decisions, to be responsible for my actions.

In the end, I hope I would have made a bit more meaningful connections with other humans, impacted them to make more meaningful connections and a bit daring about the future.

Fear and courage:

- Change in the beliefs that the other person may not understand where I am coming from.
- I would like to change my fear of "reaction" and try the other action (if I wasn't so afraid of the reaction, what would I do) more.

In terms of thoughts, that is quite interesting to ponder… because I am so action driven, I often skip the reflection or detailed planning. however, now that this question is posed, I am thinking I should consider a way to dream more, reflect more, and may have to put some inspiration board of some sort in my mind.

Dimensional Ratings: There Is a Reason
I am a very emotional being. Most of my life decisions were based on impulse—what feels right, what tugs my heart? So emotional pull has to be there for me to do things. Therefore "Compassion for Change (Emotion)" goes to the top of my list.

The purpose of this life is not about being someone but about doing the things that matter. So "Purpose for Power (Aspiration)" is my number 2.

Since I seek answers by experimentation, the starting point is usually asking myself, "What if?" And I Build. Test. And Iterate. Beginner's mindset is what makes me always be humble about the known and be more open about the unknown. So "Honesty for Humility (Thoughts)" is my number 3.

In many ways, I almost don't think about how I should influence impact. I just do. So "Influence for Impact (Behavior)" is my number 4.

One more thing!
One trait that I have developed over time is to find right partners for different projects that I initiate. I have found that to be so important. Unless I absolutely must, I always find partners when launching a project.

Before and now: Remember
Pause. Talk to your parents more. Talk to your brother more. Don't try to solve everything on your own.

****

A Life Along Watershed Decisions

Ulrich Hemel, Director of the Weltethos Institut and Founder of the Institut for Social Strategy
Born 1956. Bensheim/Bergstrasse, Germany

Ulrich Hemel was born in 1956 in Bensheim (Germany). After completing studies in Philosophy, Catholic Theology, Social and Economic Sciences he pursued an academic career (doctorate and post-doc degree). In 1991, he joined the Boston Consulting Group where he worked as a consultant in finance, high-tech, and turnaround-cases. Making a step from consulting to management, he worked as a top executive at Paul Hartmann AG where he became the CEO in 2001. In 2005 and 2013, other CEO positions in the private equity industry followed before taking responsibility as an entrepreneur with own investments. In 2018, he became the director of the Global Ethics Institute in Tübingen. At the same time, since 2017 he is the President of the Federation of Catholic Entrepreneurs in Germany. Ulrich Hemel is married, 3 children, 3 grand-children.

My life journey is a dream starting with a nightmare and coming up to a flourishing blossom. There have been many watershed moments, hard and soft choices.

My mother was both, an impressive and complicated person. She had a successful career as a journalist in the first decade after the Second World War in Southern Germany, a real exception in professional achievements in a time where women did not yet have the chances such as today. When she married my father, she converted from Lutheran to catholic faith. She gave birth to five children. I am the first of all them, and this may have contributed to being the target of a seemingly over-ambitious mother. As a matter of fact, she had redirected her professional ambition to the target of a successful family life where the children might be the extension of her own professional dreams.

The first complication in this setting has been a task of disentangling. My grandmother lived with us, and I loved her very much. The relationship between my mother and my grandmother was tense. They did not understand each other. I remember my mother saying "Hopefully, I shall never be such as my mother and all the other old-aged people." I did not like this attitude because my grandmother gave me a lot of emotional warmth.

A second complication was the parenting game which I experienced. As a small boy of five or six, I was convinced that I understand my mother far better than my father. She told me so, at least. "Do we really need him," I asked her. My father was a pleasant person, fully busy in his work as an executive manager and tired once he was at home.

The third complication was my paternal grandfather, a former school teacher with 6 children and an authoritarian style of education as usual in those times. He did not like the marriage between my father and my mother: at that time, she was protestant, glamorous, successful, not the typical rather submissive spouse taking care for home and children. The relationship between my grandfather and my mother improved over time but one of the core messages of my childhood was the saying "In your life, you can do whatever you want with one exception: never be like your grandfather is."

Confusing as it was, the real burden came from so many everyday situations which ended up with a sigh from my mother: "Another time that you behave exactly like your grandfather." For a child, this feels contradictory. Obviously, something was wrong with me. On the other side, I could not believe the truth of those harsh judgments. Thus, I took the fundamental decision to be careful about my own choices, my own way of perceiving truth, my own inner reality, my own emotions, looking for a high degree of independence from the opinion of others. I call this "***decision #1.***"

This decision made my life much easier. It helped me to take a distance from what other persons said. As a matter of fact, I have been reading a lot, often two or three books a week. In the end, I discovered the beauty of our world from both sides: from books and from nature. I really loved to take my bicycle and stroll around the river Rhine flowing close of our home.

Several years later, at the time of taking the watershed decision for a future profession, I tried to find out what would be best for doing the right thing in this world (***decision*** *#2*). I had a brilliant school career, so I had all the choices open. Reflecting about my inner motivation, my aim was a contribution to the ethical handling of technological progress. This idea was social, political, and personal at the time. Finally, I opted for a choice which seemed to combine all of these considerations. I decided to study Catholic Theology along with Social and Economic Sciences.

For this specific decision, we go back to the year 1974. The world still was full of hopes but also of concerns. There had been the years around 1968 including a strong movement against authoritarian structures in society. In a way, my decision was part of that movement, with the idea of changing a big institution "from inside." In this particular case, from "inside" meant that I had to go for a career within the Catholic Church. In the end, I decided to become a catholic priest.

This in hindsight is a complex decision with a variety of ingredients. There is a huge ambition typical for a gifted person in young age. Realistically, nobody can pretend to change the whole world or a large faith community such as the Catholic Church but it is the privilege of young persons to believe in big dreams and to go for them. At the same time, the decision was rational in the sense that I looked for a good field of action and was convinced that specifically the Catholic Church needed change, was worth the change and needed support for being able to change. There was no clear material part in the decision because such a career would not promote financial wealth but there has been a couple of emotional implications worthwhile to be pointed out.

The subsequent time in the university of Mainz and the Gregorian University in Rome have been really exciting, fully worthwhile and rich in personal encounters, friendship, intellectual stimulus, and social experience. I learned languages, took part in a homeless project in Rome, made a lot of exams, and finished at the age of 23 with two bachelors and one licentiate degree. It was time, however, to make further important decisions, both for my personal and my professional life.

Used to a critical attitude, not all details of the theological studies resulted in being convincing to me. In the end, however, I decided not to become a priest but rather aspire for an academic career in Catholic Theology (***decision*** *#3*).

On a timeline, there was a personal decision nearly at the same time but still quite independent from the professional side. On December 31,

1979, I married Susanna, an Italian girl (19) having been raised in the UK (*decision #4*). None of the both families have been very happy with this step. For my wife, building up a new life in Germany seemed to be of interest. For myself, having children early seemed to be an excellent option. We started with virtually nothing, lived in a very small apartment, were happy to welcome to life our first daughter Sabrina, and I had to look for work in a city previously completely unknown to us, Regensburg.

After a couple of months, I gained a job at the University of Regensburg, made my doctorate and my post-doc degree. It was a wonderful time, full of intellectual discussions, with the vigor of re-inventing the world. The family grew, with the second child, a son named Stefan. The emotional side, however, became more difficult. My wife became sick and was more and more unable to take care for our home. She finally decided to leave the family and go for her own paths in life.

That specific new situation came up when I was 33, in 1989. I really had to restart and reorganize my life, as a single-parent father with two kids, and as a professional at the university. My career path in academic theology was blocked exactly due to the upcoming divorce. I had to look for something else, and I decided to go to a place where the will to a positive change would be welcome instead of blocked. In order to prepare my next career path, I requested to be admitted for finance and accounting studies in the university, along with my teaching activities as a professor for religious education theory.

My contract still left me 2 years of time. First of all, however, I had to cope with my private and emotional life. A full-time job along with two children aged 6 and 9 is not an overly simple situation, especially if you consider that the job ends without any chance to continue. It is not either excellent if you consider to go for a new partnership. The decision to do so (*decision #5*) was not easy at all. It is obvious that any kind of patchwork family presents challenges of its own. It is also clear that my time budget for finding and dating a new partner would be extremely restricted.

As a matter of fact, within one year I found a very friendly, warm-hearted new partner, a German lady aged 36. After her own first marriage, Anne was looking for establishing a family, aspiring for her own child. She had the courage to leave her job and live with us as a new family. After a short time, she was pregnant, and she gave birth to Daniel, her first and only and my third child.

The stabilization of my family life was fortunate as it was not really easy to find a job where I needed to start, at age 35, like a beginner. A series of high-ranking academic degrees is not of big value if you look for a normal job.

In the end, I found a job at The Boston Consulting Group (*decision #6*). This seems to be smooth and, in a way, "brilliant" transition but it was not precisely like that for myself. The inner journey from changing the Church to working for change in profit-driven corporations is quite long. It was a systematic process with a real "revision de vie," i.e., a 360° look on my life, from past to present and future.

The following years were full of work, exciting experiences, and rewarding encounters. My professional progress, again, was very quick. I had the chance to understand a series of business fields such as finance, high-tech, and others. As the recruiting director, I had a key position within the BCG group of professionals. As the head of the restructuring case for a huge high-tech company in Germany, I gained experience and recognition. After only 5 years of professional experience, I have been proposed as a partner in BCG—a dream for all beginners, and a chance to reflect over my life.

As a matter of fact, I had come to understand that my idea of life and of contributing to changes for a better life should go beyond consultancy. I always loved taking decisions, and the consequence was another change. I started in a German family corporation having 5000 employees at that time, with the idea of making them more successful and of showing that the convergence of a humanistic approach to management and business excellence was possible (*decision #7*).

Again, a couple of really busy years were to follow. I became the CEO of that company, did a lot of M&A as well as international business. The children grew up but some other turmoil followed. The family dynamics became complicated due to a serious of reasons. Looking back, all persons involved really invested a lot of good will but the situation was simply complicated, with obvious jealousy between daughter and wife. Sometimes, it was heart-breaking because I felt torn in the middle of two hurricanes.

Finally, this time it was my own decision to separate from my second wife (*decision #8*). The burden for all persons involved had become too big. We managed, however, to do this in a respectful and peaceful way, as far as possible.

Within a short time span, important events followed at a quick pace. I had not expected to find another partner easily but life presented a surprise. An old friend of mine from Colombia asked me if I could help his sister who wanted to pass some time in Germany. I answered him positively. Incredibly enough, this sister named Amparo Lucia became my new partner, and we married with a big celebration in Colombia in January 2004 (*decision #9*).

With all these personal changes, my work did not satisfy me as much as before even if the company had grown a lot, with a much more international business and more than 10,000 employees. So, there was another change in a short time span. In a way, this has been a peak of my career because many high-ranking companies were competing to hire me. My life path was quite different, however, because at the end of summer holidays, we had a car accident in Namibia where my daughter Sabrina died, at the age of 24.

This certainly was not a decision of mine but it changed my mind. I opened my vulnerated heart and understood that I should not continue with a top management career. I therefore accepted CEO jobs in the private equity industry, with mid-sized companies between 600 and 6000 employees before I finally created my own company (*decision #10*). I still had the dream to show that a humanistic approach to business is possible, and I thought it could be better within my own company.

I stayed with this decision even if reality resulted to be more challenging than expected. I had bought a medical trade company in Germany, a furniture edge-banding company in Spain and a veneer edge-bending company in France. The world-wide financial crisis 2008/2009 met with the construction crisis in Spain, so I had to face huge losses when being obliged to sell my shares. Nevertheless, I continued during many years with the remaining medical trade company. And in our holidays, my wife Amparo and myself enjoyed travelling around the world coming to know more than 100 countries and cultures.

Two further important decisions are meaningful. When I had my 60th birthday, I decided to be friendly towards myself (*decision #11*). For other persons, this might be of little importance. Looking back, it has been nearly as important as my other self-steering decision, i.e., to make myself independent from the judgment of others, as far as possible. Before, I had been very strict and demanding with myself, leaving little time for the emotional expression of my own soul. Now, I experience much more sunshine in my life.

Another result of this fundamental or "watershed" decision is the handing over of my company to my son Stefan (*decision #12*). This was never expected but it came as a result of a long search for identity and professional fulfillment from his own side.

As a matter of fact, it has to do with a second part of the handing-over decision. I took over the direction of a university institute for business ethics in the context of the Global Ethics initiative (Weltethos-Institut). For my aspirations, this was a comeback towards my dream as a young man looking for a contribution to the ethical mastering of technical progress.

Reflecting of one's own life journey, in a way, is a challenging task. Considering "purpose," in my own life I see an answer in a contribution to healing deep wounds, both in my family and in my ethnic context as a post-war German citizen.

For me as a person, this means that I more and more open my heart for both sides, the feeling of pain and the feeling of overcoming pain and trouble by inner peace. In a word, this is the adventurous journey of love.

After more than 60 years, I already stand in the autumn of life. Autumn is a time of harvesting, and I am now more and more open to harvest all the seeds which I have been spreading. I am aware that the next steps will be steps of striving for wisdom, not in a superficial sense but in the sense of finding an equilibrium between self-care and care for others, for other persons and for other tasks. One of my challenges is to find words for all I have seen because in such a way, I can share the experience. As a consequence, I am on a path to combine aspirations and actions, even if the physical conditions for a person beyond the age of 60 do not tend to improve over time.

My main aspiration always has been to find a right way for placing my talents at the service of our today's world. This is an idealistic approach which has not changed over time. Looking at the architecture of my decision-taking for my own life, I am happy to say that I maintained my initial intuition while setting my soul free from so much emotional turmoil.

In this sense, despite all challenges, I feel like a happy person.

****

Open to Explore

Marielle Sander, Representative, United Nations Populations Fund (UNFPA), Papua New Guinea
Born 1964. Jönköping, Sweden

Marielle Sander is a development practitioner with more than two decades experience with UNDP, IOM, UNICEF and UNFPA, international NGOs, and the Swedish Government. Her career spans fighting human trafficking and labor exploitation in Eastern Europe and South-East Asia; advocacy for children's rights in Russia and promoting reproductive health and rights, focusing on women, girls and adolescents in Haiti, Eritrea, South Africa, and Papua New Guinea.

From the very start I was curious about my place in the universe. I wanted to be an astronaut, then a missionary, a lawyer and an advocate and then in an apparent about-turn the first thing I did after college was to work in film and television for a few years. I was curious about human lives and the stories we live. I wanted to experience as many lives as possible in one lifetime and movies can make that a lived reality. I think it was about what I could learn, more than what I could give back. I wanted a job that was challenging, even difficult to get. Something a little bit unusual that would also confer some status and make me special in some way. I felt some pressure to do something spectacular in order not to disappoint. I always felt a need to be prepared. Hope for the best of course but be prepared for anything. Either because my world was unstable or because I had an exaggerated desire for independence, I knew I was on my own. As a young child of 4–5 years, I had a little lunch box in the shape of a suitcase. In that suitcase I packed my most precious items: the ear that had come loose from a donkey, my favorite toy (I still have the ear); a notebook and pencil; some pictures of fairies and magical creatures. I had a sense of mission but was uncertain where it would take me. I was diligent about learning English. I began as an introvert with strong opinions but learned to be an extrovert to better navigate through my experiences.

Travels
My world has been shaped by the countries I have lived in. I was two years old when we left Sweden for Bahrain. I was nine when we emigrated to Australia; I spent my teens in Papua New Guinea, England, and Hawaii. As an adult I worked in Kyrgyzstan, Sweden, Moldova, Russia, Turkey,

Cambodia, Bangladesh, Liberia, Haiti, Eritrea, South Africa and now, completing the circle, I am back in Papua New Guinea—the country that helped crystalize my views around equality, fairness, what it means to be born a woman, and human development in general. I left my teenage years convinced and ashamed of my privilege and feeling disoriented. Somewhere between then and now, I became softer, but that was more as an act of defiance, rather than from a place of grounding. Maybe because I had done low status work (I worked as a cleaner for almost a year in Sweden while trying to break into films), and many odd jobs, I also experienced what it was like to be judged for what you do rather than who you are or what you bring to the world. I think everyone should scrub other people's toilets at some point because it teaches you something about yourself and certainly it teaches you about human nature.

Choices

After boarding school in England, I was transferred to a wonderful school in Hawaii to complete high school. On day one I was shocked to see people greet each other with hugs and cheers. At the girl's school in England, we could not touch or comfort each other. Compassion was weakness, crying was weakness, joy, creativity and/or talent was weakness. At that instant in Hawaii, I had a sudden insight that I could choose a different way of being and relating to the world. I looked at the happiness of the people around me and I wanted to be part of that, so I jettisoned anything in my personality that did not match this new world. I purged sarcasm and allowed myself to believe more in positive intent. I embraced vulnerability and a child-like wonder in being allowed to experience the joy of being in such a beautiful place. That experience has stayed with me all my life.

Identity

I had permanent residency in Australia and in my mid-twenties was pressured to become a citizen but that would entail giving up my Swedish passport, the only identity that had been a constant. Instead, I went back to Sweden to explore what it meant to be Swedish and that is where I met my future husband and father of my children. My hesitancy to commit to Australia sent me back into the arms of a Swede which eventually thrust me onto the path of international development. I had dreamed of doing meaningful work, giving back for what I had received (and correcting for what I had experienced), but working for the United Nations was a fantasy—even more remote than a career in film.

An Education

Kyrgyzstan in the mid-1990s challenged everything I believed to be true. A former state in the Soviet Union, the people there had very prescriptive rules of behavior and ways of seeing the world. I had believed that the world was ordered in the same way everywhere. In Kyrgyzstan that logic was reversed. Here, caution was weakness—cigarettes were lit beside planes being refueled—you could laugh in the face of fortune and be emboldened by skirting the arms of fate; taxi drivers drove manual cars with only one leg (true story and the handbrake was key; and International Women's Day was a genuine celebration of femininity. It was impossible to plan; why would you expect to be able to book the return date on a two-way airline ticket (after all, the future is unknowable, and things change). It was such an interesting exploration of the human psyche and so different from my own that I continue to marvel at the differences. Of course, there is more to it, but it was a good reminder of how humans shape their environment for better or worse, and that what we imbue with great meaning has no meaning at all for someone else.

Alignment

In early 2000 I was in Moldova. When I accepted a job as Head of Office for the International Organization for Migration, I suspected it would lead to the end of my marriage, but it opened the door to so much more. For the first time I felt completely in alignment with my aspirations, my beliefs, and my environment. I remember being so grateful for the opportunity to fight human trafficking and to seek justice for the women and young girls who had been so maligned, abused, and cast aside. They were migrants, I was a migrant. They were trying to make a better life for themselves, as was I. What was the difference? Only circumstance. I felt the power of purpose.

Inner voice

Moving on, in 2008 I was on the treadmill at a gym in Phnom Penh. It was my second year of a multi-year trafficking project involving the sale of organs, babies, children, and young women and men. Suddenly I couldn't do it any longer. The world had become too dark and the evil was sticky. I was overcome with the desire to end my life. This was very unlike me. It was a visceral reaction, from the core of my being. I knew I had to act and that regardless of any rational thinking, I could not continue in that position. I got off the treadmill, went to the office and resigned.

Months later I was studying for my Masters in Migration and Law at the University of London. I never regretted the decision.

I believe I am an aspirational actor. I am guided by my intuition but informed by what I have seen, learned, and understood. Material considerations are important but not a guiding principle. Being able to offer my children a good education and proper health care has been important to me and has guided many key career choices. It was only really when I came to Haiti in 2015 that I had the time to go explore my inner world. It was basically a three-year retreat in a country where I did not fully understand the language; so, to create any connection, I had to rely more on my intuition to connect with people. Apart from my work there which I found fulfilling, the people I met opened my eyes to the possibility of doing international development differently and that I was not alone in thinking along those lines.

And now...

Today I lead the efforts of a UN agency to advance reproductive health and rights—especially for girls and women across the reproductive life cycle. This is an unfinished agenda that needs the world's attention, because without owning your own body, how can you be free? If the most intimate physical aspects of your being are not your own, where do find your authentic voice? The shame and censure that girls and women must endure simply because of their ability to bear children is our collective shame as humans in the twenty-first century. The hurdles and hierarchies we construct for ourselves distract us from the real task at hand, namely, to become our highest selves and decent human. This is the lifelong lesson. I have not become. I am evolving. I believe in leaving the world a better place and I deeply believe in acting from where you stand. If you don't know what your purpose is, start by making a positive contribution from where you are now. I can't boast that I have been self-aware my whole life. I have always been curious, enterprising, and persistent. But I am also judgmental, angry, and impatient—not good qualities in a development worker. It is important for me to be kind. I think of this as a noble quest, to spread kindness and a spark of joy in unlikely situations.

WHY do you aspire to live?

My purpose is to do my little piece to make the present more livable, kinder, and fairer. I like to help people see the potential within themselves.

WHO do you feel you are as a human being?
Generally, a curious, happy soul that would like to be a better friend, sister, mother, and lover. Someone that strives to see the joy and magic in the world and can help others see it too.

WHERE do you think you are/will be in your life?
I am where I should be. And that's where I will be at the end also.

WHAT would you like to change?
I would like to complete my creative projects—send them into the universe. I would like to be more articulate and courageous in advocating for a different way of doing the work that I do now.

Dimensional ratings
Purpose for Power—1; I see purpose as a driving force for change, but without some form of power, there will be no change. Purpose is a powerful motivating force.
Honesty for Humility—2; Humility is key to compassion, curiosity, openness, and it starts will taking an honest look at yourself which is a hard thing to do, but more reason to try. Humility is an equalizer—we need more of that.
Compassion for Change—3; Honestly, it is hard to rank these four philosophies fairly. Compassion allows one to be less judgmental (important life lesson for me, I think) and to meet people where they are without judgement. With that outlook, I think it is easier for people to accept a different way of being.
Influence for Impact—4; I put this last because the others are about your own orientation to the world, beginning with you as you are on the inside. Once you have that clear, it is easier to engage authentically in influencing for change.

An advice for my younger self
Finish what you start. Believe in your ideas. Get an executive coach to work on your self-awareness and career goals in your twenties. Don't be afraid of developing a spiritual outlook. Recognize that we all begin our journey from where we stand today, and it is never too late to reorient. When you accept yourself for who you are, you will unleash your power.

****

Better Than I Could Have Ever Dreamt Of

Christian Joerg
Born 1963. Munich, Germany

An economics major from Munich University and Columbia Business School graduate, Christian has been a long time investor, senior executive, and entrepreneur founding several startups; over the last years he has been focusing on helping international founders find success in the US market through German and Ellis Accelerators and giving back to the next generation of founders as a mentor at Endeavor Miami and BUILD, an entrepreneurship program for high school students from under resourced communities He is also a member of "Better Future Network," a global group of stakeholders who focus on innovation and climate.

My journey has been more exciting and diverse than I ever dreamed of. As all journeys it has had its up and downs but I consider myself an incredibly lucky person. Personally, I grew up in a loving family and I have found love in my second marriage but I also still have a friendly relationship with my first wife; educationally and professionally, I was given opportunities in the best possible way: nothing was handed to me but I was being put in a position to achieve, if I wanted and would try hard enough…and I was lucky to have been given enough talent, intellect, ambition, and grit to make that happen against tough competition; having said that I do not consider my talents truly remarkable.

My parents, who both did not go to college, asked a "Professor" in our neighborhood, if I should attend a science-focused high school or one that still taught Greek and Latin. He suggested the latter and I did end up loving those languages and the structured way of thinking and ancient history I was exposed to by learning them. It influenced me a lot. However, for my University Diploma I chose to study economics because I wanted to live in the "real world" not an ivory tower of ancient languages. After University in Munich, I was looking for adventure and excitement beyond my home country, just taking a job or doing a Ph.D. seemed so boring; I was very curious to experience new things, always have been. I met a young professor from Columbia who was a visiting Professor in Munich while I was a student there and he encouraged my application to Columbia Business School and I managed to get an academic scholarship so I could afford it. After B-School one of my job offers was in New York and I chose that one. I have now been in the US over 30 years.

Personally, my first marriage and understanding that not the same things made us happy were very important to me, it made me more empathic about the other person's needs in a relationship. In the end I am also selfish and have a strong personality so I have to remind myself of the former. Professionally I realized at some point in my late 30s I wanted to define my success the way I saw it while before I defined success by how other people saw me or what they saw as success. I wanted to look successful rather than feel successful in my own eyes.

Choice considerations

I think the two key things are rationality and aspirations. I care about material considerations but they are a byproduct and never drive my decisions. Material comfort is a baseline but not a continuous upward driver to more, more, more. It's not a scorecard for me with my peers, at this point that scorecard is success on my terms. Emotions impact me like everyone but I try to keep them in check in the decision-making process as they don't drive good decisions in my view. I don't think much has changed over time the way I make my choices.

Probably my first professionally really challenging experience that opened my eyes as to what the senior level of business is really like and what it truly takes to achieve success; I was horribly naïve before…

WHY do you aspire to live?

I think today that is a combination of three things:

1. A fulfilling personal life in the relationship with my wife which also includes doing fun/special things together like travel to interesting locations related to history (Easter Island, Cambodia, etc.) and sports.
2. Professional success the way I define it which includes continuous learning of new things, most importantly "being part of the future" and working closely only with people I respect and trust—are "good people"—this is a lot harder than one thinks, if one wants to be successful.
3. "Giving back," working with young high school students from underprivileged backgrounds.

WHO do you feel you are as a human being?
I am a person of empathy that is generally very well liked and usually positive and helpful as a default. I am smarter than the average person but not a savant (I know some people at that level and I am not, these people are usually single minded, few da Vincis out there…). I am also somewhat selfish as I have chosen a profession where simple business outcomes and money matter and one has to contend with challenging personalities; in order to succeed in that arena, one has to make some personal and small moral compromises. Mother Theresa, I am not but I am aware of it and I am comfortable with the compromises I am making and I do not violate the boundaries I set myself. I am mildly frustrated that I do not have an off the chart's talent in some area. I am fascinated by people who have that, if it's math or skiing or tennis, such talent suggests a kind of ease which I have never had in anything.

WHERE do you think you are/will be in your life?
I think I am in a very good place as I am happy both with my romantic relationship as well as my professional situation. Frankly I hear people become supposedly "more happy/content" in their 60s and beyond…I am not sure that is true for me…I am a very active person also in terms of sports and I do not look forward to physical deterioration. I think when it ends, I will feel that it has been an interesting and probably more amazing journey than could have been expected considering what circumstances I was born into and how I grew up but I will also have to acknowledge I will most likely not have achieved something truly remarkable or outstanding. While it is hard to decide, if it had made the difference it has in a way been my "choice." To attain singular achievements in sports/politics/business one has to be willing to sacrifice everything else, my experience has taught me that. I was never willing to do that as I was too curious to experience the variety that life has to offer, so it's ok.

WHAT would you like to change?
Single mindedness of purpose would be necessary. I am not sure, however, if I am willing to make the sacrifice necessary or actually, I am…see above.

Dimensional ratings
Behavior drives outcome and in the end that's what matters. Thus, Influence for Impact goes first, followed by Purpose, Emotions, and Thought.

I think I have come to a clear assessment of myself that is realistic. The hero's dreams of my youth that were cute (like being an Astronaut or sports star) have not come true but in fairness I have achieved more than probably expected and have re-invented myself several times in that process, certainly professionally. I also have to admit that I have not been willing to make the sacrifice(s) that would have been necessary for truly remarkable achievement. From the fact that I have mentioned this a few times, one can see that it gnaws on me to some degree…yet I would not change those decisions and I am not willing to make this sacrifice now…so I think that is my personal conundrum which won't be resolved…

The importance of luck is vastly underestimated. Hard work is critical to be able to be lucky so the old saying of "the harder I work, the luckier I get" is true but yes, luck or maybe even better, timing, matters. I am an atheist after having grown up as an altar boy in the Catholic Church. That was a very positive experience with a wonderful pastor and church youth group at that time but over the years I have come to view religion as a strange human concoction to make ourselves feel better/make life seem to make sense, especially for the people that have a hard time finding meaning today/have a hard life (yes, I know that sounds like a Marx quote but, I have to say, he doesn't seem far off). Funny enough one of my best teachers in high school was a Catholic religion teacher with whom we spend many hours discussing Marx's and the Existentialists' criticism of religion…

I love to read "serious" science fiction literature. I am 100% convinced we are not alone in the universe and we are at the lower end of intellectual evolution with many beings out there of vastly higher intelligence who potentially might lead a purely "thought" existence, soul/brain uploaded into machines (as we might eventually). General AI will soon outpace human intelligence and possibly benevolent AI will rule the world as humans are way too imperfect to continue to drive the correct decisions and will eventually be replaced in the decision-making process.

An advice to my younger self-

Very interesting that I do not have a great answer for this. I think I needed to go through my own learning, not sure any advice would have helped…

****

My North Star

Joan Ai, Founder of "Prepared Child"

Born 1975. Shanghai, China

Joan Ai is a mission-driven corporate social impact and digital purpose advisor and entrepreneur at the nexus of corporate social responsibility (CSR), innovation, and technology, with a focus on the social implications of technological change. She was a Fellow at the World Economic Forum (Seconded by DQ Institute), where she worked with corporate, government and civic leaders as well as academic experts to increase digital intelligence ("DQ") literacy, citizenship, and readiness in children and adults, especially those in marginalized and underserved communities. Her work helped to close the digital gap between the 53% of the world's population that was online and the remaining 47% that was still offline (pre-pandemic). Her start-up Prepared Child is a member of the NYU Steinhardt Edtech Incubator (powered by StartEd).

"From everyone who has been given much, much will be demanded; and from the one who has been entrusted with much, much more will be asked" (Luke 12:48).

First and foremost, I am an immigrant with a deep sense of her family background and history with tremendous empathy for the immigrant experience—the trials, pain, struggle, hardship, and hope for endless potential. The experiences I encountered as a child and my family upbringing served as the basis of my values and deep sense of purpose.

I have been blessed to have come from a unique family background from Shanghai and this pride has been the backbone of how I was proudly raised. Our family that at one point were the governors of a major port city in China (Ningbo) and lived next door to the Mayor of Shanghai then came to America and lived in one of the poorest areas in New York City. At the height of the pandemic in 2020 when New York City was the epicenter of the COVID-19 crisis in the US, Corona, Queens had been the hardest hit area in the entire city.

There were many instances of my grandmother, mother, and me being taken advantage of because we were a family of three females fearlessly navigating a new country, a radically different culture, and having to make ends meet or catch-up because bills had to be paid. We struggled and carried on with only our dignity and sheer pride and determination to remain in this country because it truly was the land of new beginnings and opportunity. All of these experiences made me aware that I had to not only stand up for myself, but also for others as I always had the self-awareness to do so because it was fair and the right thing to do. How does one channel all that history and insight into two entirely different worlds; leveling the playing field to benefit the most marginalized populations?

Following my heart: My professional path

If you asked the 10-year-old Joan what she would be doing when she grew up, she would have told you that I would be a lawyer and possibly pursuing a career in public service. I was determined to follow in my grandfather's footsteps and had developed a rigid checklist and timeline for what I needed to accomplish every step of the way. The 10-year-old Joan would not have been able to understand that life not only gets in the way to thwart your plans, but it conspires to make sure that you listen to your heart to understand your life's path. For a young immigrant with a strong overachiever personality, there is no second outcome or pathway. What you set out to do is the answer to your happiness and there is only one defined path. Yes, one understands the mechanics that life can get in the way, but the 10-year-old Joan would have found a way to maneuver around it so that she could achieve her goals according to the schedule she had set for herself.

Looking back now, my life has been a collection of all the time I spent committed to doing the things that gave me joy and a sense of fulfillment—something that the 10-year-old Joan would not understand and would most likely have caused her great confusion. It's taken me 45 years to come to realize that the more time I spent trying to resist listening to my heart the more problems I encountered. The more I tried to adhere to my checklist and timeline, the more I was thrown off. I discovered that when I didn't feel excited or fulfilled in my work, the Universe would conspire to disrupt my life in some way that brought me on to the next part of my journey whether I was ready for it (or not).

This started early for me when I interned at two law firms and was immediately turned off the legal profession. There was nothing I could do to get me to be excited and I quickly realized that I had to come up with a Plan B. Unfortunately, I had spent my entire life leading up to college with Plan A so I had to rewrite my script, but didn't know where to start. My mind didn't know where to start…

I graduated from college without script. I started off in my first job as an IT consultant at Accenture with the goal of moving to Shanghai (for the growth and opportunity the market offered in 1998). After Y2K,

I moved on to working in investor relations at chinadotcom corporation (NASDAQ: CHINA). While I wasn't physically based in China, I was working with a Chinese company and there was opportunity for me to move abroad. My dream of moving to China did not transpire due to personal reasons with my family, but I never regretted my decision to stay home because being close to my family meant more to me than moving abroad. Soon after the dot-com bubble burst and everyone in our 100-person US operation (except my boss who was the head of investor relations) got laid off. I was moving onto my third career in three years—I had my "quarter life crisis" and I needed to find something that I would be passionate about and stick with it (or at least for a few years).

I randomly stumbled upon the corporate social responsibility (CSR) sector one day while reading a dot-com industry newsletter. I was deeply moved by what this woman had written about her field and it made me very curious to find out more about the work and also to get hired onto her team. I never realized that this would be the catalyst for my successful 15+ years career in CSR at three major global Fortune 250 companies—giving me solid experience and understanding of how major corporations operate and having the opportunity to help people find purpose and meaning through volunteerism, but also to direct millions of dollars into the nonprofit world. I thrived under the fast pace environment at these companies; helping people to give back and to identify causes and issues that were most dear to them and to help channel their energies for good. I enjoyed developing narratives for our work (during the nascent stages of the CSR/ESG sectors) and how employee engagement and volunteerism helped shape and contribute to company culture. I loved the creativity and level of freedom I was given because I had mentors and bosses who cared about my professional development and helped set a high bar for me to understand the importance of leadership and paying it forward. I was incredibly blessed to have had all of these people and opportunities in my life—I rose to every challenge and pushed myself harder each time and held myself to an extremely high standard of excellence. However, I took the time to share my learnings and made some great friends along the way. I loved being a team player and for me it was all about loyalty, gratitude, and having a hard work ethic. I worked hard and I played hard too! It was the perfect balance for me.

Fifteen years later this all came to a screeching halt when I disrupted my personal and professional life. I got divorced and left my career in CSR, embarking on a period of voluntary solitude to contemplate my life's purpose. I was emotionally exhausted and for the first time felt that the work I was doing no longer held the same meaning and that I was a hypocrite for trying to advance something that I once loved doing which felt hollow. I had hit a personal and professional wall and the only thing that I knew I could do was to take a break.

After a summer focused on healing, an idea came to me. My purpose was to focus on my child—his happiness and upbringing were my priority and as a single parent I was determined that I would provide him with all the tools he needed to live a life of meaning, purpose, and happiness. However, I also needed to think about my next professional challenge and to continue to contribute to a greater good.

My north star: My prepared child

I never imagined that by being inspired by my child (and following my heart) that it would lead me to the next chapter of my professional development in the innovation and entrepreneurship space. My experience in the start-up space was very different from the first time I had been in it during the dot-com bubble of the late 1990s. This time, almost 20 years later, I was a start-up founder and no longer working for a publicly traded company. My start-up, Prepared Child (a B2B SaaS platform to engage children to be socially conscious, philanthropic, and purposeful) had been accepted into the NYU Steinhardt EdTech Incubator and I was immersed in the entrepreneurship ecosystem. No longer working in the corporate space; I was now engaged with Gen-Z college students, start-up founders (of all ages), venture capitalists, industry leaders, and everyone else who made up the start-up ecosystem. I had never felt more alive and wanting to absorb information and to learn about all the exciting innovation that was being developed. This time I was part of the wave and I knew how to keep my head above water and to enjoy being swept along for the ride. It was glorious.

I didn't succumb to "imposter syndrome," but there were many times during the rollercoaster of emotions that any start-up founder inevitably goes through—the steep learning curve, the "fish out of water" feeling; where I had gone from a traditional corporate job into the start-up (university) world—doubt, hesitation, fear of the unknown, and decision to bootstrap or explore VC funding—all of these were questions that I constantly pondered and that I knew that I would not have an explanation for right away. So, I pushed everything aside and decided to let go and allow things to take a natural course. I was extremely proud of my long track record in CSR, I was an informed parent, and I was determined that my social impact start-up would have relevance in helping other children in the digital age. I would focus my product on the industry that I knew best (corporations) so while everyone else sold to school systems, I pitched to my corporate network. I developed my product with the sole intent—not only would I "eat my own dog food" (as they say in the start-up world), but would I feed it to my own child? It was critical to me that I built with love and purpose.

Pivoting & Pirouetting

I would never have imagined that all my work on Prepared Child would then lead me to a 14-month-long fellowship at the World Economic Forum (Forum). I never worked harder my entire professional career than when I was at the Forum. I was given unimaginable access to thought leaders and experts in all different industries, and it was there that I discovered what I am best at and where I shine the brightest.

I have been blessed with many talents, but what I enjoy most is to tackle thorny subjects, develop a strategy, define the narrative and identify the leaders and get their buy-in so that they may come together to co-create the solutions necessary to address critical global issues. I love setting the stage by making a compelling case to individuals and managing the process from conception, delivery all the way through implementation—and I know that I can do this at scale. I am creative and enjoy using non-traditional means to achieve my goals so that the journey is never boring. I am also naturally curious about many subject areas so for me it is not the cause, but more if I feel that I can make a difference. As a result of my extensive experience, I am not deterred by hard work, the challenges that may arise or maintaining a positive attitude in the face of adversity because everything becomes a learning experience and is opportunity for growth.

My next chapter & Raison D'Etre

It has taken me 45 years to figure out who I am—personally and professionally—and how the two are inextricably intertwined and have made me who I am today. At the time of this writing, I am in search of my next chapter. Wherever I land I know that I have much to be grateful for and I still have a lot of "unfinished business" that I am seeking to accomplish. I have never had a stronger sense of purpose where I want to channel all my lived experience, compassion, and insight to do good. We have one life and I choose to live it with intention, passion, and humility. Regardless of the number of days I have ahead to look forward to, I know that I am also raising a child that will have a strong sense of purpose and responsibility. My son is my family's legacy and while I respect his individuality, I have also taken the lessons that I have learned to help give him more guidance so that he can live his life smarter, better, and be more assured. I hope that I have imbued him with a sense of duty, gratitude, and conviction to always do right by others and to leave the world a better place than he found it because not only do I expect it of him, but his ancestors demand it.

****

Legacies

Erastus Mong'are, Founder and CEO for StartUpAfrica Inc.
Born 1971. Kisii Cunty, Kenya

Erastus Mong'are is the founder and CEO of StartUp Africa Inc, an international non-profit organization that supports African youth in the building of business skills and in endeavors that foster financial independence, create jobs, and grow African economies. As CEO, he mobilizes people and resources to support development projects in Africa including initiating partnerships for entrepreneurship initiatives. His vision is to work with others to impact the lives of 10 million youth through entrepreneurship by 2030. He is a recipient of numerous awards including Kenya's Presidential Head of State Commendation (HSC) Award, Delaware's Governor's Proclamation, Public Allies Delaware Changemaker Award, Tomorrow Leaders Today Award for Community Service, and Distinguished Toastmasters Award among others. For more information about StartUpAfrica, visit www.startupafrica.org.

WHY are you here?
What I do today in the community to give back is influenced by my parents, Mr. and Mrs. Jason Mong'are. My father is now deceased (dating when I was 14 years old), but the actions I saw him and my mom take (feeding the hungry, housing people in our tiny home, helping them find employment in the tea plantation where he was a supervisor, giving clothes from the few he owned, and being the go-to person for community issues among others) would have to be the foundation of the person I am today.

Many years later, I, a child of a tea plantation worker who didn't even make $20 a month, could find myself in the US having arrived here for college education. Months into being here, a story in a local newspaper about shooting by some teens would send me in search of answers, and eventually, being introduced to volunteerism at a local Boys and Girls Club, and later, an award, "Tomorrow Leaders Today" that opened doors for me to get an opportunity to serve as an AmeriCorps member through Public Allies Delaware. The experience could change me totally, and the ethic of service has become part and parcel of my why, seeing me as a solution bank for issues, rallying people to support, and address them.

WHO are you?
I can describe myself in many ways, but as I think through, my personality has been shaped by where I was born (growing up in the tea plantation with little made me realize that life isn't all about material things, but about relationships with people, neighbors helping neighbors), my parents teaching about honesty and taking responsibility for my actions and grades in school, their actions helping others have built in me compassion and an understanding heart that helps me see other people's needs and through them, I am able to relate very well with others. Tied to this, I am one person that can get along with others, because at the end of the day, I know that we all need each other.

The work I do is not for the impatient, but those who like marathon runners realize that to get to the finish line, one needs drive and determination to keep pushing even when you want to stop and exit the race. I make running part of my weekly running routine because it helps me understand that, if I can have the patience to complete 10 miles running, then whatever challenge I am dealing with at work or in my personal life can be overcome with patience.

Finally, my personal life and work have been guided by the ability to be courageous. Growing up in Kenya as small boys, we would venture into a deep forest in search of wild fruits and honey unafraid of the danger that loomed. That courage and losing my father at an early age, being in unknown situations, not sure of what tomorrow brings has always helped me do what's right in difficult situations.

WHERE are/will you be in life?
My life and careers have been shaped by my place of birth and where I got early years of education (nursery to high school) in Kenya, and later coming to the US for my university studies and first job. As the founder of StartUpAfrica which I manage today, I do it an enriched person from different worlds and different experiences. I believe these have helped me

approach my work and service in ways that in my view are geared towards collective impact, togetherness, and community.

What would you like to change?
As a leader, I am aware that my actions towards the success I wish to see in others and the organization I run requires that I do proper planning, seek resources, and communicate among other actions which will in turn bring the results that will influence the future as I see it.

I sum up my pro-active stance in life with these two personal quotes:

"If you're a volunteer, that's what you are-a volunteer, you get out and serve." Erastus Mong'are.

"The best advice I ever got came from my dad a day before he died. He told me, 'Learn to be around people.'" Erastus Mong'are.

I am living and keeping my parent's legacy alive—they served, they modeled, they impacted lives. I give that in return for my world.

****

Follow Your Curiosity

Andi Cuddington, facilitator by day, kitchen dance party enthusiast by night, traveler by heart
Born 1984. Vancouver, Canada

Andi strongly identifies as "West Coaster" despite living all over the world. She earned a BSc in Neuroscience from the University of British Columbia and an MSc in Social Psychology from the London School of Economics. She is passionate about creating space for conversations that count. Andi draws on her background in neuroscience, systems-thinking and creativity problem-solving to design processes and experiences that promote exploration, open dialogue and, most importantly, change. You will always find her armed with sharpies and post-its, ready to move the pieces around on a challenge.

When I tell my life story, I like to reinforce the idea of "wonky paths" as a way to remind people that we don't necessarily know, in a linear way, what leads to what. I often use the metaphor of collecting dots. When you're gathering moments, experiences, jobs, travels, and people, it's like it's a scatterplot that doesn't necessarily make sense. But if you give it enough time, the connections form and the dots create a pattern that you didn't see before. Slowly and patiently, they make a constellation.

The plot twists

Like any good story, there have been a few plot twists where an event marks a unique or important change of course on which narrative (and character) developments depend. I've agonized over a few momentous decisions that now seem small when I put pen to paper but I think we all have experienced the smallness of big moments in our life once we've passed through them. Below are four transformative moments that shaped my journey and my perspective on the world.

1. Switching Universities
   Feeling a bit cowardly because I "couldn't hack it," I was aware that needed to break free from how I anticipated university to be but I didn't know how. The decision to switch universities after second year was made in a split second after months of rumination. As I stared out a window on a train speeding from Munich to Venice, a cosmic sign emerged on the horizon. Yes, just like a cheesy movie. In the distance, a second train was snaking along with a single blue freight car with the letters UBC stenciled on the side. These were both the colors and the abbreviation of the university I transferred to—the next month I moved back home to complete my degree at the University of British Columbia.
2. Backpacking in Africa for five months
   After finishing university, I wanted to travel and see the world. In the early 2000s, the common graduation trip was to load up backpack and get a working holiday visa for Australia. But for a bit of the surprise (nay shock) factor, I opted to forego the typical Aussie adventure and headed to Africa. The decision to backpack solo for six months in southern and eastern Africa as a 20-year-old woman was far less common than it is now. I couldn't even find someone who had traversed the lower half of the continent. That trip monumentally grew my sense of independence and changed how I understood the world and my privilege.
3. Experiencing the "pit of despair"
   I think we do a disservice to ourselves and our narratives when we fail to honor that big changes often emerge from life's yucky moments. It's the danger of keeping up with Jones or matching the gloss of Insta-lives. The deepest despair I've known came in my early 30s, when my three best friends became pregnant with their first babies within a nine-month window. It felt like they were moving

on, proudly joining a new elite club that I was not a member of, and I felt excluded.

The weight was crushing. Red-blotchy faces from crying were hidden by a polished mask that said "I've got this." No one except my mom knew that I wasn't doing well at all. Eventually, I simply got tired of crying every day. Even though crying only takes 17 muscles, it is a full-body experience. I was exhausted. As the deluge of daily tears receded, I could feel that the whole paradigm needed to shift so that I could pull my overbaked "life cake" out of the oven.

I started to see the breadth and depth of the things I could do with my life again. My aperture on life fully re-opened once I started the THNK School of Creative Leadership which became my intellectual baby. The thing that I could nurture, that could consume all my waking hours and some of my sleeping ones, that would shift my self-identity. THNK gave me a reinvigorated sense of learning, inspired me to design bigger dreams bespoke for me.

4. Striking out on my 18-month global "working sabbatical"
   It was during my time at the THNK School of Creative Leadership that I met my 80-year-old alter ego. And she knew that I needed to get out of my comfort zone and be re-inspired in my life, both personally and professionally. If I wasn't going to be doing life according to the official "white picket fence" statute, what else did I want to be doing? Professionally, I had spent the last ten years facilitating complex change in the health sector (what a mouthful) and I was attempting to figure out what I wanted to be NEXT when I grew up. Broadening my horizons and exploring would be a tonic for both.

Jobs fill your pockets. Adventures fill your soul. The formula for my working sabbatical was simple: 4 countries, 4 months each 4 different jobs. Unlike other more traditional sabbaticals, this year wasn't about pressing pause on my life. It was designed to accelerate change and growth, personally and professionally. I was listening to that small voice inside, asking me to see what else is out there.

Even now, the magic of how that grand adventure miraculously came together still surprises me. The crazy idea to "prototype my life" taught me how to experiment, ask for help and stoked a fledgling faith that things work out. (If you know me well, you know I often utter the quote "everything works out in the end. If it hasn't worked out it, it's not the end"). No matter what, it was a daunting step to take. Unknowns and what-ifs abound. Making big life changes are pretty scary. But you know what is scarier? Regret.

Two guiding questions

Consciously, my life has been guided by two main questions: "Does this seem interesting?" and "Will I learn something?" But to pretend that my choices are so precise and my decision-making process so exacting would obscure the true story. Subconsciously, it's a complicated tango of emotions and rationality battling over who will lead, combined with a shadowy attachment to material success... all of this is set on the stage of my unrelenting and uncompromising desire to do good in the world.

Even from a young age, big decisions danced through three phases. You've seen a bit of that in earlier questions but I'll unpack here. First, I make lists of the pros and cons till kingdom come, pretending that rationality will save me. But as long as the decision stays in my head, I can easily rationalize both sides since hard decisions are either a comprise between two good choices or two equally bad ones. Next comes a period of waiting, where I just sit with the question. During this time, my heart is holding space for the two versions of my life that could unfold. This phase has been the hardest one to honor because it takes forever and there is nothing I can do to speed it up. Eventually, it is my gut who is the decision-maker and, without pause, one option shines above the other.

What has changed over time is that I've become more confident in the stages of my process. I'm better at holding space for it now than when I was younger... back when I believed in "right decisions." Now I do a simple thought exercise that can help me speed through some of my fear that creates decision purgatory. I imagine I'm eighty, sitting in a rocking chair and reflecting back over the years. What would I have done more or less of? It helps me check that I'm living a colorful and creative life.

WHEN did an experience completely change your beliefs?

I'm not sure I've ever completely changed my beliefs but that is probably because my beliefs are constantly evolving that I don't notice how much they've shifted over time. Even as I write this, I can see some of those shifts in the stories captured here.

WHY do you aspire to live (What is your Purpose)?
I've long struggled with the idea of a single, life-affirming *Passion*... as my good friend Debbie says "we're living in the tyranny of the passion people" but I'll leave that essay for another time. *Purpose* is a bit less fraught but I still struggle with the singularity with which we frame it as if one is better than having many. Casting modern-day society's attachment to passion and purpose aside, my motto is "follow your curiosity." When I've gotten off-track in life, it's usually because I've forgotten this simple mantra.

When I'm looking for the "red thread" that connects many of my different experiences into a constellation, it is the desire to belong. Belonging is symbolic to me because it was a piece of my life that was in flux a lot in my formative years. Creating spaces where other people can find their tribe of magicians and misfits is a gift I can give wholeheartedly because it matches a yearning of mine. It's the reason I build communities.

WHO do you feel you are as a human being?
I think the best way I can share how I feel as a human is to describe the scene above my desk. There's a big bulletin board filled with little pieces of nostalgia—a collection of favorite photos, birthday cards, and little sentimental notes. One note, shaped like a luggage tag from a friend who is a curiosity advocate, says, "What does your heart say?" There is a pin that says "I'm library people." Next to a birthday card from my mom with purple sea-stars on the front (and I love the symbolism of sea-stars for resilience) is a card from my dad that says "No worries for next ½ mile." Below it a tattered Queen of Hearts (I collect those when I find them on the street blowing in the wind). An old business card that says "Let's talk to strangers" (it harkens back to one of my first experiments in permission granting). A conference name tag where we got to invent our ideal job title (mine was Idea Astronaut at the Ministry of Inquiry). A post-it wishing me well at my new job. Tucked in the top corner is Nora Roberts quote that says "Magic exists. Who can doubt it when they see rainbows and wildflowers, heat the music of the wind and the silence of the stars."

What this board says to me is that I appreciate the warmth of human connections, of memories, of the time spent together. To me, this is what makes life feel meaningful.

WHERE do you think you are/will be in your life?
A friend of mine introduced me to an alternative version of the hero's journey called the Virgin's Promise that feels like a pretty good descriptor of where I'm at. In this version, the virgin is the feminine youth (though not always female) who must find her own identity and path separate from the one her home confines her to and, in so doing, transforms both herself and her kingdom. This framing resonated with me because it is both transgressive and transformative.

Right now, I feel like I'm in the first stage of this journey in my life right now—whether it's the Call to Adventure (in the hero's journey) or the Opportunity to Shine (from the Virgin's promise). I can feel something big brewing in the tips of my toes.

But when it all ends, I will be telling stories, probably around a campfire, with people I love.

WHAT would you like to change?
Despite feeling pretty aligned in my emotions, thought, and actions most days, the scale of the impact—my ambition—still feels too small, making my sense of alignment a bit like a fractal. If I fully believed that the world was conspiring on my behalf, the risks I would likely be taking were even bigger than the ones I take now.

In the near future, I'd like to actually make something of my own (but maybe not ON my own!)—to put one of my many ideas out into the world. To do that I would have to put a stake in the ground and that's scary. But I've shed the cloak of comfort once before so I'm ready to do it all over again.

Dimensional ratings
For me, my values are what anchor my aspiration as well as the way I engage with the world. I've learned to lean into my intuition and emotion as a helpful guide because they give more texture and context to the abundance of thoughts in my overactive brain.

****

Purpose Without Action Is Daydreaming

John Roche, SAP Advisor, USA
Born 1964. Providence, RI, USA

John Roche is an advisor with SAP and an experienced leader for digital transformation to connect people, things, and businesses to run the world better. He helps CEOs and business leaders to define their vision and leverage digital trends to transform their company. He provides guidance to CTOs and enterprise architects on end-to-end architecture design. Connect with John on LinkedIn.

My life's journey until now has been a constant expansion of mind and body generated by a continuous stream of good and bad experiences. I have always had a plan for my life since my teen years but instantly "throw away" the plan when someone or something enters my life that I feel I must pursue even if it goes against the plan. This has opened my life to people, places, and things that I would have never met or experienced if I had stuck to my plan. Those interactions and experiences have continuously shaped the person I have become and the person I am still becoming.

There have been several watershed moments
One of the most significant was the summer I met the woman that would become my wife. I had just graduated from university and I went to visit my sister who had moved to Ireland. Although I had a well worked out plan for the next five years of my life after graduation, the plan did not include meeting that woman. The feeling I developed for this woman that summer made me realize I could not walk away and not have her part of my life, so I asked her to marry me instead. This is the first of many situations where I would forgo my plan when I felt a stronger pull to go in a different direction. Another significant watershed moment was the decision to relocate from a good paying job in Boston, MA to the 25% unemployment rate in the rural town life of the West of Ireland. At 26, with a wife and two small children, there was no safety net and survival was key. I failed early and often before I succeeded and managed to run my own business and support myself and my family. This experience expanded my mind and my relationships and developed a confidence in me that took away the fear of failure which would be a valuable asset as my life progressed.

As regards to what influences my choices
In my early adult years, my choices were influenced by aspirations (to make a difference) and emotions (it felt right) over rationality or material considerations. However, as I aged and became ultimately co-responsible for our five children, I had to balance aspirations and emotions with rationality and material considerations (i.e., beyond basic needs, the money needed for healthcare, education, etc.).

Sometimes, an experience can completely change your beliefs
My mother was diagnosed with cancer when I was twelve years old and died when I was seventeen. This shattered many beliefs I had at that time with regards to how life worked. Another experience that completely changed my belief was on September 11, 2001. Up until that day, terrorism at that scale had only ever existed in my mind in faraway places where the people were fighting thousands year old wars. It was never something that had touched my world. It was the first time I feared for the world my children would grow up to live in.

WHY do you aspire to live?
My purpose in life is to connect each day with as many people as possible and to have as many experiences as I can fit into each day. Going through the experience of my mother's death at an early age gave me a very different view on life than most of my friends. I saw life as fragile and fleeting and something to be cherished every day. There have been many adult people in my childhood and teenage years that provided me with advice and guidance during and after that experience that caused me to form the opinion that my purpose in life is not to live a long life but to live a good life for as long as it lasts. That means starting each day grateful that you awoke and that you are alive, going for a walk to appreciate the world you live in, saying hello to strangers, bringing a smile to another person's face, listening to a person in need, smelling the air, thankful at night for the day that you had and praying for another tomorrow.

WHO do you feel you are as a human being?
As a human being, I believe I am the sum of my relationships. Today I am a husband to one, a father to five, a grandfather to one, a brother to three, a cousin to dozens, and a friend to many.

WHERE do you think you are/will be in your life?
I am probably 2/3 of the way through my life journey. No one really knows where they are in their life's journey as they can no more predict the end than they could prevent the start. Of course, it is possible to force the end by harming oneself. But that action aside, and assuming I do not fall foul to a major illness or accident, I expect I am 2/3 of the way through my life's journey. I hope when it ends, I will be in a place of love surrounded by as many of those I have loved as possible.

WHAT would you like to change to fully align your aspirations, emotions, thoughts, and action?
Of course, it is never too late to change course if I feel I am not proceeding in the desired direction. I am continuously learning and traveling to stay aware of what is relevant currently to avoid living in the past and I am working to change my work role to be in a position to have greater (positive) impact on societal issues of the current day.

Dimensional ratings
If you do not have a purpose, you have no starting point. However, purpose without action is daydreaming. For the action to be meaningful, you must have thought. Passion is always a good thing and with the other three is like "icing on a cake."

An advice my younger self?

Don't worry so much…it might never happen 😊

****

Crises Require Change

Almuth von Below-Neufeldt, Retired member of the lower saxony state parliament
Born 1954. Hamburg, Germany

From 1961 to 1974 I attended school and graduated with A-levels. When I was 15, I was in Washington with my American letter girlfriend for 6 weeks. 1974–1978 I studied, graduated in clothing engineering (FH). Thereafter assistant to the management (clothing industry) and from 1981 official of the labour inspectorate, from the chief inspector (handling) to the director (head of the authority over 7 years); part-time lecturer at study institutes, administrative colleges, etc., *also in the construction of*

East after the reunification. From 2009 to 2017, I had a mandate as a member of parliament in the Lower Saxony State Parliament. private: 1991 Marriage to Herwig Neufeldt, hobbies: my horses (driving, breeding) and dogs; Mountain holidays in East Tyrol since 1958!

In me there is still the will to improve things that can be changed. I have many ideas for this, so I give some and implement some, overall driven by a very strong life motor. But I also have a special ability: I am a courageous woman. Someone who speaks to me in a period of despair will get hope and perspective. My father could do that, and so can I.

I have been committed and successful in my career; forgetting about my commitment and self-defined duties—or what I think of as enjoying life. Being now almost 67 years old I would have deserved that long ago!

Watershed moments

My father was good-natured, smart, committed, and successful. He gave me strength; but it was also the death of my father that deeply and permanently shook me and my life. I was a really good student until the day when I found him dead. To be left alone in that situation, with the police, the press, and various organizational issues to tackle, that was a burden beyond the possibilities of the girl who had been protected until then. It triggered a veritable descent; there was no help. Not from the mother, who acted unimpressed—I had always relieved her of any burden thus far, so she expected this arrangement to continue. Time would soften everything. My feeling, my distress, that nothingness, did not take place. To absorb the resulting downfall of my performance has cost me decades of life and enormous will and energy; because I could not start professionally as I wanted. Eventually I managed to make the necessary course-corrections; without a well-meaning sponsor, but with immense effort and work; and the complete deferral of private interests. Too high a price.

Perhaps it is precisely through these experiences that I am so keen to value people around me and in my team; to meet them fairly and in a supportive way and to give them perspective as much as I can.

There was a shift in my decision-making, from the heart to the mind. As a young girl I decided professionally what I could do and what I had fun with, so my choices were very much influenced by my emotions. Later, I corrected that course: I told myself that I had to make great progress in my career so that I could afford what had always been my dream. I managed to do this, with rational decisions and huge effort. In that period, I also bought my first horse. The friendly cool black mare gives me much joy and connection. Opening up horizons she was life-affirming and changing my daily leisure life! She is the basis of my tribe and the small horse breeding on my own farm.

But there was another turning point in my life: my cancer. Until then, I trusted in a way that appears as naïve from today's point of view. I've learned that life is finite, moments are unmanageable, and life can be over very quickly. With a very sensitive antenna, I now notice with great sadness when people die, often very quickly and quite unpredictably in my vicinity. Also, in the past, when I couldn't walk one of my favorite paths during a holiday, couldn't reach a favorite place, then I always thought—well, then next time. Today I think of such places or paths with the thought of whether I will ever be there again, and there are many destinations that I miss. For example, the high mountains of East Tyrol will remain precious memories, because I will not be able to get there anymore. My consolation is that I know the great feeling of having reached the place and will never forget it.

My place today is still mentally controlled by the motivation to implement a new way of cooperation between bosses, superiors, and employees. It takes shape in an initiative for good, for better work: SeeU. SeeU is important to me. Examples from my professional practice illustrate Why:

A family man and the main earner applied for special leave without pay. He was granted it. As a direct manager, I was informed about this after returning from my holiday and asked why the employee wanted special leave. The reasons were not known. I asked in the quorum—the man had a seriously ill wife and wanted to take care of her and his young children. I made sure he moved to the home office. With salary. About 25 years ago that was a more than extraordinary decision!

A single father was criticized by his manager because he was often not at work during the prescribed attendance period, and often came too late in the morning. It turned out that the morning family life demanded such an increased time requirement that an individually agreed extended flexitime immediately ensured satisfaction between the manager and the employee.

A woman in the family phase could only work part-time. She had however immense potential. Though she could manage the targeted courses organizationally, she was not able to do any further testing. Allowing her to do training on the job in various stages with different institutions that were part of the SeeU network resulted in very positively evaluations; thus, paving her path for higher-level tasks which she became very successful at.

I'm trying to get people to adopt this idea—which entails a new culture of leadership and also the end of some convenience. New requirements for superiors must become mandatory! Incidentally, this must also become the content of studies. Professional competence is fine, leadership competence is absolutely important, but it requires a lot of empathy. Compassion is a hither blind spot in all trainings. Here is an example:

I was the new woman, a married woman around the age of 40, and had to go to the office of my new colleague and superior of about the same age, who sat at his desk. I stood in front of his desk like a first-grader. He listed my future task cut, then threw the summarizing page towards me, which sank beyond the desk edge to the floor. I didn't repeal. It was in my mailbox the next day. A few years later, I successfully applied for a chief executive position.

Let's see where my path still leads. The end is far from near. I am still looking for a way to ensure more emancipation in working life: in my opinion, no one really takes on this very big task in a systematic and targeted way: to make women step into their competence, with their experiences and skills, to make their ideas heard, to value their opinions as significant, and to reflect them in the company culture. Conscious steps, appreciative for the woman, enriching for the team, and beneficial for the institution/business can change that.

Good work, trade unions are campaigning to do just that. It would be nice if it were true. I really want good work. Fair pay is one of them. Applause for essential workers in Corona times really doesn't help! Recognition means decent pay. You have to be able to let go of old times procedures! If one believes satisfaction interviews with employees, factors such as appreciation, recognition, praise, justice, holiday entitlement, professional development are at the top of the value scale. Why is there not also equal pay for men's and women's work?

On March 10, 2021 was the Equal pay day. In my view, it is a scandal that women earn so much less than men in the same position/task that they work without pay until today.

Appreciating women in the workplace, the right step must be taken as a matter of urgency. SeeU would be a good approach to get started. Good work cannot mean that mothers with the double burden of job and family are the first to square the circle. Our society only exists when there are children. They are enriching for everyone, especially in their families.

Employers must accept, appreciate, and take accountability for the balance of private and personal lives of all their employees.

WHY are you here?
My purpose in life is to do good where it is possible for me—so I want to make the world a little better and set new impulses.

Even when I was at my lowest points—my commitment, my reliability, and my attitude to live on were never taken away from me: I have been and remain committed to making things better. When I say things, I stand for them. In the coexistence with others, I seek to help; offering them opportunities to do what I think is great; or a possibility to share with them to do what I think is beautiful. I encourage, comfort, cheer, formulate concerns or use my contacts to convey something positive. For example, at work that may have meant practical retirement support for staff. Sometimes I simply invite someone to a good place, e.g., on my farm or in the high mountains.

WHO are you?
I am friendly, curious, hardworking, and communicative, my loved ones are always on my loved ones. So, I see myself as a caretaker and enabler, and I am generous, reliable, and creative.

Often, I am a counsellor or supporter, I plan and act consistently. Ideas do not get stuck in the field of dreaming, but are realized. In my professional career, I paid attention to error prevention and constructive quick solutions in terms of task completion, thus being a modernizer and networker. In terms of personnel management, I was appreciative, skills- and career enhancing, and helpful to distressed individuals. During my time at the Government, I tried to lift my peers out of the trough of "so it has always been" by designing training courses combined with executive coaching, regarding new media; whilst promoting cooperation with other sectors such as universities and economic players.

WHERE do you stand in life?
I am in the middle of life, even if the years of professional activity are already over; I am often perceived and driven. When my life ends, I'll say it's a shame, I needed more time.

Ultimately however my life illustrates that we, I, have to allow myself to think and live "me first" myself. Otherwise, we pay the price. There is no top and bottom, no subject to make that happen; no arbiter but myself to allow me that space. Taking that perspective is good for me, and the organization that I am part of. All assigned positions serve the whole, that would not be reached without the individual. So everyone is valuable in the place where they work. Instructions and controls are necessary instruments, not that I am misunderstood. Imagine the alternative, if people are not doing their job: What if no one picks up the garbage, what if no one works in the crematorium, no one repairs the smelly sewage pipe or installs the garage door or tars and paves the road, clears the snow, etc. Boundaries exist. The measure of responsibility is and remains very different. That's why not everyone has to earn the same, not everyone has to be my friend, and have insight into my private life. But arrogance was yesterday. I expect appreciation and respect from everyone for everyone.

WHAT would you like to change?
I take time out with my horses, dogs, or in the garden. Then I think in peace and quiet without any external distraction.

At the same time, I want to initiate, in the very first step, the beginning of a large-scale change in an appreciative world of work with respect in mutual interaction. Employees must not be seen as mere providers of services and recipients of benefits and time, but valued in their personality—and that also means that individual requirements are made possible. Attention to individuals benefits everyone and has a positive, motivating, identity-creating effect in the company; which is success-enhancing, and I am convinced, makes the company more successful in recruiting the best minds?!

Dimensional ranking
Finding meaning: 4—because I have found my purpose; even though there is still room for development! Emotion: 3—this is important, especially empathy—but the head and rational decision-making also play a major role in finding good and feasible solutions, if that is necessary, purely emotional decisions cannot be made and something can be advanced. Humility/honesty 1—nothing works without trust and honesty, without humility and acceptance for the thoughts of others, then putting my values and emotions on top would be like a wet or scratchy sweater—this leads to discomfort in the next person and not to well-being. Influence of effect/behavior: 2—because the first impression is unrepeatable. If you know this, you also have to recognize that your own doing, being, speaking can open doors and hearts or close them forever.

The advice to my young self
would have been to invest more and earlier in skills than in mobility. Life consists of time. Giving and using it well must be considered as a priority, even at a young age; it is finite and unrepeatable. Spending a lifetime commuting (i.e., a long distance from home to work) and spending a lot of time on work can only mean a short investment period for a worthwhile perspective.

Professional success must be in balance with life, work is important and especially good when it is done gladly. But work is not everything. It is only part of life, but an important one.

****

My Life's Journey So Far

Gareth Owen, Humanitarian Director of Save the Children UK, London, UK

Born 1968. Kettering, England

"Born in Kettering, England in 1968. Gareth Owen has been the Humanitarian Director of Save the Children UK since 2007 and has spent the past three decades responding to major emergencies all over the world. A civil engineer by training, he is passionate about collaboration and leadership and was a co-creator of The START Network, Elrha and The Humanitarian Leadership Academy. In 2013 he was awarded on OBE for services to emergency response abroad. Gareth currently lives in north London but returns to his beloved Wales as often as he can."

When I was a young boy, in 1970s suburban England, I wanted to be a train driver. I would stand on the bridge at Sonning Cutting, hand hewn by Irish "navigators" for Isambard Kingdom Brunel's Great Western Railway, and wave at the speeding Intercity 125s as they charged back and forth from London. If I was lucky, I'd get a deafening "nee-naw" siren whistle from the driver. Movement, journeying, travelling fast, to my childhood imagination the commuting passengers had a serious purpose that I wished to emulate.

Imbued from a young age with a sense of responsibility for the world at large and to care for those less fortunate, my two older sisters and I had been taught to always clear our supper plates and to be grateful for our good fortune when so many went hungry in the world. My mother worked night shifts at The Royal Berkshire Hospital and my father was an academic who taught tropical agriculture at Reading University to students from all over the world. From an early age our house was full of impossibly exotic folk, speaking in strange accents, bringing small gifts from distant homelands. Undoubtedly, I idolized my father's achievements. We had a huge Times World Atlas that would be fetched out every time he made an overseas trip so that we could trace the length of his latest journey across the pages with small fingers. I longed to roam the globe doing good deeds as he did.

Love, kindness, compassion and a sense of responsibility towards others formed a deep well of foundational values that I would constantly draw on throughout my life, though I was yet to really discover my true motivation in seeking to become a humanitarian aid worker. That eventually happened by accident.

I would summarize my life's journey thus far as a series of happy coincidences, involuntary twists and intentional turns that led down new paths of discovery and adventure. A journey of emotional growth from joy or adversity and perpetual motion: initially studying hard at school and learning life lessons from tough team sports like rugby, the agony of adolescence and late development, going off the rails and failing crucial exams, re-sitting and scraping into university, stumbling sexual awakenings and miserably unrequited love, a detested first job, further studies, first overseas trip. Minor watershed moments of a life beginning to find direction, mostly influenced by blurry, ill-formed personal aspiration and parentally infused rational intent, mixed with youthful defiance and impetuosity. In a word: normality. And then a life-changing decision of the most abnormal kind.

The watershed moment

In January 1993, at the tender age of 24, I volunteered to go to Somalia as a humanitarian aid worker. This decision was the one true watershed moment in my life. Until that point, I was a conventional middle class British kid, dreaming of living an interesting and fulfilling life. I had never been hugely driven by material wealth—mine had been a modestly comfortable upbringing, though money was tight enough for us to be quite frugal as a family. There were no holidays abroad, rather we would return at every opportunity to Wales, and my parents had been unable to afford the banjo I yearned to learn at the age of eight. But the second I set foot in Mogadishu my life became a tumbling cascade of watershed moments. A US-led foreign invasion to relieve a famine was underway and I found myself in the thick of the action. I handled a lethal weapon that first day in Mogadishu and wondered how much death it had dealt.

Twenty-four hours later I stood for the first time in a feeding center for severely malnourished adults in Baidoa, one of the first of its kind since the Second World War. It rendered me speechless. I had stumbled into hell on earth. Nothing in my previous twenty-four years of comfortable existence could have prepared me for this moment. I stood rigid, frozen to the spot in shock, transfixed by the abomination of malnutrition. Suddenly lightheaded, wrestling a rising gorge, I was consumed with a powerful fatigue, bewildered by the tragedy's immensity and burning with outrage at the seemingly callous indifference of humanity towards so many of its precious own. In one moment, my life was changed forever. It was an experience that completely change my beliefs: henceforth I would lead a life dominated by powerful base emotions. It would take many years and some incredible coaching to really learn how to firstly contend with and later positively channel the true power of that moment in Baidoa.

Barely a week later I had my first brush with death when my vehicle narrowly missed a landmine while scouting the deep Somali bush. Within a month an expatriate colleague had been shot dead on the same dangerous stretch of road between Mogadishu and Baidoa that I'd also travelled on first arrival. But for fate, it could easily have been my own short life murderously curtailed. The cascade would become a giant humanitarian waterfall of life moments that continued in the years ahead.

I left Somalia soon after the infamous Battle of Mogadishu, immortalized by Hollywood in the movie, "Black Hawk Down," and was reassigned to the city of Malange in Angola. It was one of Africa's dirtiest post-colonial conflicts that had embroiled superpowers during the Cold War and became a brutal civil war fueled by oil and diamonds. The story of my time there is a story of heroic missionaries, ruthlessly efficient South African mercenaries, medieval siege tactics, inhuman starvation and personal descent into near madness. We barely escaped with our own lives having saved thousands of others from death. By now I was very damaged. Today it would be called PTSD and I would receive help, back then I was merely burnt out and in need of rest. I sought my own counsel from a psychologist friend who told me the one thing that I needed to hear: it was okay to no longer be the same person who had left Reading eighteen months earlier. How could I possibly be? But still I felt a terrible sense of selfish failure. My altruism had been self-serving and my loved ones had borne the brunt of worry.

I watched as my colleagues from Angola battled cholera in Goma and felt a complete failure. The guilt I felt at not being "tough enough" to see out my two-year volunteer contract in the midst of genocide was the most bitter moment of my short life. The rapid cascade of life moments had tumbled me to the bottom of a deep, dark, ice-cold pool of personal despair. I was left to wander the wilderness of my bleak thoughts for half a year before I found solace again as a volunteer in the Himalayas.

And so, the tumbling waterfall continued. I rose up again in Uganda, where I met the love of my life. We journeyed together to Kosovo and Gujarat before returning to the UK where I joined Save the Children UK in January 2002. There have been many more life moments since—the highs of achievement and the lows of tragedy.

What influenced my choices?

In my early twenties a close friend strongly recommended a book called "The Road Less Travelled" by Dr. M. Scott Peck. My friend had experienced a terrible accident while travelling abroad and the book had helped him come to terms with trauma. Though it did not immediately grab me, the book was my first foray into alternative notions of personal growth through love, suffering and hardship, life purpose and spirituality. Though I only paid scant attention at the time, looking back I can see that it had gently blown on kindlings of deeper thoughts within, awakening an inner flame that would only truly reach the surface of my consciousness after decades of humanitarian endeavor and the loss of a primary emotional anchor—my mother.

Alice Jane Owen was a person of deep religious conviction, though she never tried to persuade her children to be the same. In any case, to her mind I was "doing God's work" and it was my choice. I did not know it at the time, but I was glimpsing the formidable power of the unconditional love for humanity that my mother had so freely given right up to her death from cancer. I had been filled with her boundless love and now it began to spill forth, as if her passing broke a dam in my soul. Now it sits in me like a white-hot furnace beneath cooling ocean depths of peaceful contemplation, ready to be directly tapped whenever needed. Though my mother is no longer physically in my life, her influence on how I relate to others has never been stronger. The enormous comfort I draw from that is impossible to describe in words.

My father continues with his life, now in its ninth decade. A man of stoic character, he keeps his emotions mostly hidden and shows us his love in myriad practical ways. He spends his days in contemplative routine, mowing the considerable lawns on the family farmstead, listening to his beloved Welsh language in song and verse, reminiscing of his hard, but idyllic, early life on a small hill farm in border country, organizing charitable activities, usefully contributing to the community around him as he has always done. I observe his busy energy, its effervescence slowly fading, with admiration and wonder and still seek to emulate his life travels. Does my own contribution come close to matching up to that of my parents I often wonder?

What is my life purpose?
Over time, the weight of emotion driving me relentlessly on has shifted to a deeper plane within. I am no longer contemplating the next phase of immediate action in the next war or disaster. I still find myself motivated to act by the same profoundly humanistic considerations, but these days my actions take a different, more politically minded form. So long as there are people on earth there will be conflict. Humanity has sadly not evolved away from violence, far from it. Indeed, the world seems to have entered another dark phase of history. We live in the Anthropocene age, where the actions of humans will determine the fate of the whole planet and all its inhabitants, where "necropolitics" endures and where late-capitalism is untethered from the liberal order that restrained it to wreak havoc like a disease, creating untold inequality and misery. We humans seem to have learned very little from our own history.

So my purpose in life remains the same: to make as positive a contribution to the cause of human solidarity as I can muster, one that would make my loved ones proud. As a human being I feel vulnerable, flawed and prone to mistakes. It is undoubtedly true that there have been times in my life when my selfish actions have hurt others and I feel bad about that. But latterly I have learned to offer myself the same unconditional love and compassion that I have tended to show others. I am trying hard to live a good life, free from the excessive greed of late modernity and learning to let go of guilt attached to past events.

How do I define myself?
I was recently asked why I continue to strive to save and protect all human life. After some thought I found myself turning to cosmology for the answer: for us to exist it took the creation of our universe around 13.7 billion years ago, the formation of our own galaxy, the stars, the

planets and by some miracle of the universe the creation of life itself on earth, from which we have evolved over countless millions of years. To waste even one human life, therefore, is to wantonly discard what all of known time has produced. When my own time on earth draws towards an end, I want the satisfaction of being able to say, despite all the challenges the world faces, giving in to human despair was never an option I had much entertained. So I define myself thus: I am a pragmatic realist who is stubbornly and abundantly hopeful for humanity.

Where will I be when It ends?
There are already enough anecdotes and memories in my life to fill one of the beautiful mountain lakes of Snowdonia in my beloved Wales and I wouldn't change a thing about the life I have led. Perhaps I will write it all down one day and contemplate its meaning while mowing the grass on the family homestead where I write these words. When my time finally comes, I'll be buried next to my parents in Saron Chapel graveyard overlooking the stunning rolling vista of mid-Wales. I hope my epitaph will read, "here lies a kindly man who tried his best for humanity."

How would I rate the four life-philosophies?
I would rate "compassion for change" as the most important life philosophy, followed by "honesty for humility," "purpose for power" and "influence for impact" in that order. As I have become older, and hopefully somewhat wiser, I have realized that compassion is a beautiful gift we can always offer to self and others and when coupled with humility, sense of purpose and kind behavior greatness is possible.

Advice to my younger self
I would tell my younger self to always be a giver not a taker, default to trust, be kind to everyone, including yourself, listen first and seek to really comprehend, overcome your fear of connecting with your own emotions and those of others and find the courage to always express what you are truly feeling.

****

Shifting by Degrees

Randah Taher, Culture Designer and Innovation Facilitator, United Arab Emirates (UAE)
Born 1977. Arabo-Canadian

Randah Taher is a Culture Designer and Innovation Facilitator with a playful sandbox. In it, there are methods that design cultures of innovation, creative problem-solving sessions, biomimic analogies, design thinking bootcamps, edutainment games, and creativity tools. A TEDx and keynote speaker on creative environments in organizations. By understanding people's ways of thinking, cultivating their talents through improved processes, facilitating different innovation methodologies, and designing programs that fit the proposed challenges, she works with organizations and mavericks to nurture the smallest cultural shifts with the biggest impact. Her bottom-top approach helped translate ideas into multi-disciplinary programs as well as develop internal innovation functions. From The "Creative Institute for Toronto's Young Leaders," to the Montreal-based crowd-sourced nonprofit powerhouse "My Arabic Story," to the design-led innovation consultancy "sajory" with its programs, and curated subscription box "IMAGINESS by sajory" in Dubai. These are but a few examples of the stories she shares.

In 1977, I was born to proud Palestinian parents who had witnessed the horror of Nakba and ethnic cleansing, yet never once showed their trauma. They raised us intentionally in safety, security, and home where they shared stories of love for humanity and of kindness to one another. Jordan became a home for my mother's family while my father was based in Austria. Yet they came back together in another land.

My sisters and I were born in Saudi Arabia, whose culture I grew to love in so many ways: friends, music, sense of humor, and most of all its dialect which I fully embraced. When my father passed away in 1997, we carried his legacy with us to Canada, a place I called home for the next decade of my life. Having studied, worked, and started my family there, I consider myself a very proud Arab-Canadian.

Who am I today? I am Palestinian blood, Saudi dialect, Canadian brain, and a loving heart. What about you? Let's talk. randah.taher@gmail.com.

My life's journey goes through waves of confidence and confusion. These waves are very normal and expected. I started to notice the signs and patterns of when the tide comes in (confidence) and when it starts to retreat (confusion) and I embraced the interplay between them.

As a child, I didn't want to confine to cultural norms or follow an existing path to how one lives. I chose to do things my way. To experiment and take on adventures as a way to find out who I was and why am I here in this world. I realized early that I didn't want to be labeled within an existing category with other people.

My career followed this thought process. Although I stayed to my truth and took on jobs that helped me bring on my full self while helping others reach their own destination, they were always an experiment in time or a phase in the journey. I therefore switched my job roles every 12 months, despite staying with the same organization for years. I didn't want to repeat the same experiment twice and expect to learn something new and so I chose to advance my career horizontally, rather than vertically.

The first watershed moment of my life turned me around 180 degrees
From being a highly dependent person on others' laying the ground before me to becoming fully independent in how I design my own path. When my father died suddenly with a heart attack, I was too young to realize how this will shape me forever. Although my grief lasted a year, I matured and turned my life around. I started making conscious decisions about everything around me, and that's the moment when I realized my father's comment when he mentioned how being stubborn actually helps me achieve any goal I set my mind to.

I married my best friend. That phase in life was an augmentation of where I was going and how expanded my universe is. I was starting my professional career and feeling confident about it. As soon as my first-born son arrived, I switched character again. Never was I more consumed of someone's safety and protection outside my own body. It changed the way I show up in my work and how I embrace opportunities. It was the reason why I started my first organization in Montreal and how I learned to be more patient and plan for long term. I also took more calculated risks. Something I didn't need to do before.

Fast forward a few years of life, moving cities for work and welcoming my daughter into this world, I found myself dealing with new circumstances. I was well-aligned when I continued my Masters study and applied what I learned at a job that extended its impact to the boundaries of the City of Toronto. I didn't know it at the time, but that was a moment of full confidence and growth that lasted around 18 months.

Once I reached that height, I started searching for a new confusion to embrace.

We decided, as a family, to explore the world and I decided as an individual to try for a new career.

I challenged myself to find an opportunity in a sector I haven't explored before. I applied to different jobs and found myself accepting one that not only gave me a new geographic location, but it was also in a field I did not read a book about, yet. A totally new experiment and a completely new game rules with a whole lot of unknowns. It was exactly what I needed, when I needed it.

I moved to the UAE to teach at the Architecture Engineering Department in one of the local universities in the country. I lead student courses and projects in a unique way that could only be offered by the only non-architect instructor in the faculty. Breaking rules again. Not conforming to cultural tradition, again. The short-term confusion led to a speedy growth in confidence level as I embraced my new position, skillset, and unique angle on living my life purpose within the university borders.

Choice considerations

I believe at every phase in my life my choices were influenced by more than one of the 4 dimensions at the same time. At the transition of any phase, I made decisions based on what was needed the most in my life at the time. Here are some examples.

When it came to starting my business after my work with the university, aspirations and rationality played a big role. I was trying to find the connection between what I wanted to do in my life (my legacy) and what the world needed at that moment in time. There was a lot of thinking and a lot of experimentation and feedback insights.

When it was finding the right place to live (or the city to move to), material consideration was the highest priority. We were trying to address the sensations we wanted to feel from living in different cities and neighborhoods and with different temperature (the weather as well as the cultural aspect). It is not a surprise to others that I can shifting my living room design with small tweaks every single month. It gave me enough energy and stimulation to look at the same possessions I had in new lighting, and inspiring my thinking thereon.

Raising children and showing up for family (and all the choices fed into that decision) were set entirely by emotions. Work shifted from part time to full time and back again depending on where my kids (three by now) were in their journeys. I was lucky enough to control some of my working hours (through my career and not necessarily for each job) and I took advantage of that, knowing that my kids will only be children for a short amount of time. I wanted to be a visible part of their upbringing and create those memories together.

Traveling as a family was geared not only by emotions but also material consideration as well as aspirations as each one of my family members embraced their own individual search for their purpose in life. They opened up their minds to other ways of living and sought knowledge that went beyond books or screens.

My restless personality could not allow me to stay at home and settle. This would have eaten my desire to find myself, away from family, and share my talent with the world. My aspiration to be part of the work force was pulling me in all sorts of way, from paid, to volunteer, to project-based engagements. I always chose the adventures that helped my brain expand in new horizons. I was moved by all dimensions of POZE at the transition periods between confidence and confusions.

While I have multiple experiences that switched the way I see life,
one of them was my travel adventure to the amazons, at the starting tip in Ecuador.

I went alone for self-discovery and the need to add stimulation to my thought process. I came back with new conviction on how we survive in different worlds yet maintain similar levels of happiness. I overcame my anxiety of finding bugs in my backyard by becoming an intruder in the bugs' own backyard. Seeing how small we are as humans compared to the majesty of the forest changed my view on everything.

During that trip, I was bitten by a bug. It was so fast that we didn't even see what bit me yet left its mark with two teeth, one centimeter apart in the palm of my hand. The pain was so intense it shot out of my ears and being in the middle of nowhere meant I have only two choices, continue walking towards the river (our original plan) or go back to basecamp 2 hours away.

I decided to continue towards the river.

10 minutes in as we walked through uncharted territory of the amazons. My friend and guide who is also a tree doctor found what looked me like any other tree. He sliced a small patch of its surface and out came a bright orange thick liquid that mesmerized me. I anointed my hand with this natural cream and within 60 seconds all signs of a bite, swollen hand, and pain had disappeared instantly.

It was magic.

That moment between me and this tree switched my mind to refocus my energy on finding ways to learn from it and apply its lessons into my world. The tree has been my mentor for so long, but now it is part of my life.

WHY do you aspire to live?
I knew I was a natural problem solver and that ideas come to mind like popcorn in my head. I thought everyone shared this skill. Until I realized they didn't or don't know how to use it effectively.

I found my greatest strength in helping others get ideas as fluent as I did. I started by providing helpful inspiration sources and that lead into training on ideation tools. My studies, work experiences, and volunteer projects have honed my skills that feed into my life purpose: to help people find their creative selves again, even after years of battered down minds with old-style schooling and ripped-out-of-creativity workplaces.

WHO do you feel you are as a human being?
I am who I am because of the unique experiences I lived with my parents, family, extended family, my travels, and the cities I explored. I am a curious and social person who enjoys connecting with and learning from those who have a unique perspective on life. As a refused to be labeled into a pre-existing category I try not to judge others before listening to them. I'm open to new ways of living and new ways of working. I appreciate the circular economy because of its use of creativity as well as revolving around the community and not the one-person dimension. I don't believe there's only one way to solve problems since we have so many neurons in our head to be used and reused.

WHERE do you think you are/will be in your life?
At the moment I find myself at a crossroad. I believe I'm ready to take on the world and ride the confidence wave. I wonder how my purpose will fit with the overall purposes of the communities I wish to serve. I'm curious about my next direction, my next experiment in life, where would that lead me, and what impact am I creating and leaving behind.

Everything I have accomplished and experiences I witnessed so far has led me to where I am in this moment. The accumulated wisdom is taking me by the hand to where I need to go. Staying a bit longer with ambiguity is a skill I developed along the way and one I fully embrace. I know it's not a permanent condition, nothing is, but each step we take leads us to a distinct journey.

WHAT would you like to change?
We go into waves of alignment and misalignment (or confidence and confusion) that connects our aspirations, emotions, thoughts, and actions at different phases in time. It's perfectly normal to find ourselves sometimes not knowing what to do or how to do it even if we feel confident about our decisions. I trust that it's only a matter of time when I re-align all dimensions in a way that makes me confident, powerful, and of service to others.

I believe that any step I take, in whatever direction, will lead me to find the details of the other dimensions. If I put myself in new circumstances, by physically being somewhere else or experiencing with a new sense, I'll be able to figure out what's my next step. If I connect with others in a way that I haven't done so before, it will make it easier to align our mutual aspirations. If we think collectively and measure our actions with the way we make others feel then we are able to see where in this world we need to be next and thus take actions towards it. It's one foot in front of the other, or one arm stroke after the other, regardless of the starting point.

Dimensional ratings
Going to the roots of a problem, before coming up with ideas as potential solutions, helps in addressing the right pain point rather than the symptoms or the shallow surface. In my line of work, nurturing a culture of innovation is the root of the problems of keeping talented individuals onboard and creating continuous improvements on services and products at the same time as we improve the process, or the how we do what we do.

This leads me to consider "Honesty for Humility" as the most important first step simply because it embraces all four interrelated dimensions. It brings on board the soul, heart, mind, and body that correspond to the four arenas in which we invest our energy in: growth, love, work, and play.

Once we establish the foundation, we build the connections with each other and support our "Compassion for Change." When people in a team or an organization have a sense of belonging, feel truly valued and engaged, they connect better with each other as well as within themselves. The individuals find a way to relate their own aspirations to the purpose of the organization they are a part of.

"Influence for Impact" comes next. When a group feels strong and well connected, they become aware of their decision-making process and how it impacts the work they do as well as each other's lives. They are inspired by those who are well-aligned and start developing the structures that will support their ambitions to be aligned as well. New behavioral patterns emerge when everyone make better decisions for themselves as well as their teams and experimental learning nourish the feedback loop. At this point, certain individuals will pause to have a second look at their own selves and decide if they are serving their own purpose in life or need to find another group or another situation to support. Then the "Purpose for Power" comes in with a full intentional mind and courage to develop and nurture our own aspirations to feed into our everyday living.

I would tell my younger self,
to trust its own creativity that she will figure things out at every confusing corner she will experience. When the pain is too strong or when we are so confused about everything, that is exactly the moment when our brains are open to learn how to lead the way. It requires time and being gentle with ourselves rather than hurry to solve the shallow problem just to quiet our minds. I would tell her that not knowing is part of the journey, so embracing it will help find the short cut. Taking the time to discover and explore is her right and she needs to make it part of her journey to do things on her own, at her own terms with zero guilt carried along. It's part of life and part of growing up. Take those steps, one day at a time and you will make it work beautifully.

****

From Growth to Change to (m)Equilibrium

Andrew Shatte, Co-founder in Chief knowledge officer meQuilibrium
Born 1962. Brisbane, Australia

Andrew is a fellow at the Brookings Institution's Center for Executive Education, a former professor of psychology at the University of Pennsylvania and currently on the faculty of the College of Medicine at the University of Arizona. He has published prolifically in peer-reviewed journals and is the author of The Resilience Factor: 7 Keys to Finding Your Inner Strength and Overcoming Life's Hurdles and meQuilibrium 14 Days to Cooler, Calmer, and Happier. Shatté has trained hundreds of thousands of professionals over the past two decades to build their own resilience and coping skills, with demonstrated success in bringing about long-term change in productivity and performance. He completed his undergraduate education in his native Australia, and completed his Ph.D. in psychology at the University of Pennsylvania, where he worked on the first programs in positive psychology. A highly acclaimed teacher and TED presenter, Shatté is a sought-after speaker.

For as long as I can remember, I've been a very ambitious person. At every stage in my life I've been significantly more ambitious than the baseline of those around me. If I utilize POZE as the framework by which to view my life, I would conclude that I've been primarily motivated by Purpose for Power.

I was born into a working-class neighborhood in Australia. We did not have paved roads, we did not have indoor plumbing, we did not have money. My father worked for the government and my mother was a stay-at-home mom so we had very few monetary resources. Suburbs in my home town of Brisbane were rated annually on their quality on a scale of 0–100 and my suburb never reached double figures. The temperament of the neighborhood was one of—complacency. People accepted their station in life. They accepted that this was their lot in life and could see no way out. Many people have an illusion of control—perceiving control where it doesn't exist. But those in my neighborhood had an illusion of lack of control; failing to see how they could improve their lives and failing to take initiative.

I believe that it was a very fortunate, accident of life that I was born the youngest of three and youngest by a wide margin; my sister is 9 years older than I and my brother 12. This meant I had to work very hard intellectually to keep up with the family or else get left behind in conversations and activities. I couldn't keep up with my siblings on physical strength or speed but I had a chance to match them on "smarts." And so it was that intelligence became of paramount importance to me. I saw it as my ticket out.

I excelled academically. I was nakedly ambitious with everything academic. I would get up at 4 in the morning even in grade school to study. I became perfectionistic. Any grade short of 100% was unacceptable to me. If I received a grade of 99% I totally ignored the 99% correct and drilled into the 1% in which I'd "failed." It paid off. I was valedictorian in every grade in elementary school through high school. As my elementary school education (culminating in 7th grade) was drawing to a close I looked for ways out of the 2 high schools into which my neighborhood fed, knowing that they would set low bars. I won a scholarship to a private high school where I knew my aspirations could be fulfilled as it would be the perfect launch pad into a quality university. It was.

I was accepted into the study of law. My future seemed all set. It's difficult to recount the sheer amount of work that went into getting myself out of the gravitational pull of my neighborhood destiny. I had worked countless hours to achieve academic perfection. From the age of 8 I was "shunned" by my peers for devoting myself to study; something that simply was not done where I came from. I was 17 years old and about to embark on a law degree that would guarantee me the respect of my society and the material comfort and safety I had desired from childhood. Within 18 months, everything changed.

I despised the study of the law. It became remarkably clear that I did not want to study it and I did not want to practice it. So now I was faced with a dilemma—adhere to my ambitions or surrender them to be true to myself. I chose to drop out of law school. In the rearview mirror, through the lens of POZE, I can see that I unconsciously realized that the pursuit of power (i.e., being a successful lawyer) was futile if not married with a sense of purpose. I needed to find something meaningful to devote my career to. Fortunately for me, I found psychology.

Watershed moments

There have been several that are easily subsumed under the POZE model.

1. When I was around 10 years old, a decision was made to put a six-lane freeway through land around 100 meters from our house. The noise was overwhelming. The freeway obviously jagged far from wealthy suburbs in order to snake its way through poor neighborhoods like ours. To me the message was clear; rich people had power and a voice. Poor people had no power, no influence, no voice, and no ability to control their lives. This was a bifurcated lesson for me. In the POZE model, it was the first time I was really in touch with my sense of injustice, the emotion it caused, and how it drove my behavior for control (striving for achievement in education). I was focused on the Emotion and the emotion as an impetus for change. But it also taught me a lesson in helplessness—that often we are at the mercy of forces beyond our control. This was the first time I can recall where I first explored the boundaries of locus of control.

2. After I graduated from college with a degree in philosophy and political science, I got a job in the Australian government, Department of Social Security. It was my job to interview people who'd been downsized or fired from their jobs. Some were able to get up from the setback, dust themselves off, stand up in the face of this adversity, and get motivated to find a job. Others fell into hopelessness and helplessness. The differentiator was resilience. This began my lifetime fascination with psychology and, specifically, the study of resilience. The year was 1984. I've been diving into resilience ever since.
3. In late 1985, I'd spent a year working towards a degree in psychology—a full-time job and studying 6 courses in psychology at night. On a whim I left Australia for Tokyo, Japan. I had just turned 23 years old. I intended to stay for 2 weeks. I stayed 3 years. Both the decision to go to Japan and the decision to stay were very Emotion-based decisions. I believe it was the first time in my life when I had made any important, and certainly life-changing, decision because of how I felt. I was always a very rational and logical person. I looked down on people who made emotionally charged decisions or who justified their behavior by telling me "that's just how I feel." Now I was doing it—knowingly. And I knew that it was the right decision.
4. There is another reason why this was a watershed time for me. It was the first time in my life when I wasn't near the power apex of the society in which I lived. Sure, I was poor. But I was white, male, and heterosexual. Now suddenly I was a minority and was the object of racial prejudice. It was eye-opening for me. It transformed how I saw social dynamics; race & gender. It fueled in me a sense of social justice that was now experiential in nature and not just academic. I always reasoned racial prejudice was wrong, but now I felt it was wrong. And so it proved to be another POZE example—how I had wed the emotional/experiential side of the equation to the cognitive/rational beliefs I'd had all along.

Choice considerations

My choices have traditionally been made under rationality but completely in the service of aspiration. That is, I saw logic and reason as the best way to make decisions that would further my aspirations.

There were notable exceptions to this—my decision to go and to stay in Japan as mentioned previously. But there are many more decisions made by rationality/aspiration even at the expense of emotional drives. I neglected friendships and intimate relationships to achieve my ambitions. I chose a graduate school based on what would advance my ambitions, knowing that such choice went against what I knew was the right option for me emotionally (would make me happier, would lead to more joyful work).

In the background was always the drive for material possessions, although I've always known that for me it was much more about material safety than ownership of the things themselves. But it was never front and center.

I believe that once I had children the weighting shifted. One may believe one is making decisions about one's children based on rationality but, if one were honest, one would be forced to concede that all decisions made about children are emotional decisions. And as a provider to 2 small humans who cannot provide for themselves, my ability to guarantee their material health and wellbeing—to provide them with "things"—took material considerations from background to foreground.

A small event with massive consequences for me

I was in college and at a party at a friend's house with my college girlfriend, almost 40 years ago now. My friend said something which angered me greatly. What he said is lost in the mists of time—I honestly don't remember. But I remember I fell into anger which was an all too familiar state for me. Anger is my signature emotion. I have never been a very emotional person, but of the 7 negative emotions that get in the way of people's lives, anger has been mine. So, on this occasion, my friend obviously said something which I perceived as a violation of my rights. I grabbed my girlfriend's hand and told her we were leaving. She asked why. I told her. In exasperated tones she explained to me that I had misconstrued what he'd said. That when he said X, I had interpreted it as a slight when in fact it was not. In that moment I knew she was right. In that moment I had a memory rush of incidents that were similar; where I had imagined a violation of my rights. This changed everything for me. I no longer perceived that the world and everyone in it was out to get me. Instead, I realized that I had developed a way of scanning the world where I looked for violations until I found one, real or not. This was my first experience with the great Greek Stoic philosopher Epictetus who said, "we are disturbed not by events but by the view we take of events." This was the basis of my theory of Emotion Radars as the causal beliefs in our emotional life. It was my first notable experience with the fallibility of human thought. In the POZE framework, it helped me see there was a Rational dimension to the Emotional.

WHY do you aspire to live?

This has changed over time. Until my late 20s it was ambition; to succeed to the very fullest extent of my ability in my academic pursuits and in my career. As my career developed, it became more important to me that what I did contributed to the greater good. I made decisions where I worked on less high-profile projects for less money in order to do something that would help (e.g., help at risk children avoid depression, help college students manage the transition into college, help corporate employees succeed, train the military in resilience in order to, hopefully, save lives).

Those forces still remain but they've been greatly superseded by my role as a parent. My children give me my purpose. Watching them develop, guiding their learning, helping them achieve resilience are more important to me than all else. There are times I carve out time for me or my career, but I can't help but feel it pales in importance compared to the work I do as a Dad. This week, for example, I ran several webinars and town hall meetings for corporate employees on resilience. But what gave me the most meaning was the 9 hours I spent trying to recapture my son's pet rat after it escaped its cage.

WHO do you feel you are as a human being?

Once upon a time I could not have answered this question, as I saw my job title as being the essence of who I am. I'm honored to do a lot of work with the military, including combat veterans who were involved in multiple firefights in Iraq and/or Afghanistan. They all tell me the same thing. In those moments when everyone's life is on the line, everything but your very essence strips away. Rank doesn't matter—you're no more protected as a captain than as a private soldier. Age, race, gender—none of it matters. You see yourself for your most essential characteristics.

I have never been in that situation. But if I try to imagine what I am at core, I believe I would say smart, curious, entranced by complex connections between pieces of information, warm, gregarious, humble (but with enough arrogance that I want people to know I'm smart and successful), driven by the desire to be funny, to make people feel at home.

However, I also acknowledge I'm a work in progress and that at times the better parts of me are overtaken by anger, anxiety, greed, envy, jealousy, and pridefulness.

WHERE do you think you are/will be in your life?
I do not believe I'm as far along as I need to be in my aspirations, cognitive development, emotional development, nor moral development. I'm 58 years old. The average life expectancy in the U.S. is 78. I have another 20 years before "the end." I'm 74% through. Even if one allows for the fact that our development really doesn't begin until we're 20, I'm half way through.

I don't know where I'll be "when it ends." I do know where I hope to be. I'm reminded of the great work of psychologist Erik Erikson and his 8 ages of man. For Erikson, all of our social, moral, and psychological development is wrapped up in the final stage; ego integrity versus ego despair. Do we end life with the feeling (Belief & Emotion!) that it was a life well lived, that we did what we could, that we served a greater purpose? Or does life end in despair in the knowledge that we have not actualized our potential, missed significant opportunities to do good. I have experience with each in both my professional and personal life. I have seen people go out with integrity and some with despair. It's already front of mind for me that I should work now on ensuring ego integrity.

WHAT would you like to change?
At this point in my life, I'm trying to operate out of a mindset of plenty versus a mindset of paucity/poverty. The latter leads us to zero-sum thinking and action. The former leads to positive-sum thinking and action; where one believes that rising tide lifts all boats. It's our baser instincts that lead to zero-sum competition—millennia of evolution that, to paraphrase Thomas Hobbes, wired us to be nasty and brutish towards one another. My ambitious and competitive nature, forged in the fires of my childhood neighborhood, can get in the way of this for me. I'm led into feelings of envy and jealousy which are manifestations of zero-sum thinking—that another's success is my failure.

I aspire to be positive-sum and to embrace a growth mindset for myself and others.

My zero-sum thoughts lead to negative emotions that threaten to derail that aspiration.

I need to continue to challenge those thoughts, debunk those emotions, and act in ways that deliver on the aspirational promise.

Dimensional ratings
I still believe that our aspirations are like the north star—they set the trajectory of our live and determine how we navigate day in and day out.

Following our Aspiration (contribution, purpose, values, goals) comes Thought. My career has been spent demonstrating the power of thought; that the thinking styles we develop determine what we feel and what we do. I have come to acknowledge the power of human emotion in directing our decisions. I believe we often make emotional decisions and then, subconsciously, wrap the decision up in a rational veneer. But they are emotion-based decisions just the same, regardless of how we choose to dress them up.

And finally, behavior. I placed this last because I believe that behavior is the net and determined result of our Aspirations, Thoughts, & Emotions. Behavior is almost the inevitable output of those other processes.

An advice to my younger self
You worry too much. Understand your sphere of influence; what you can control and what you cannot. Understand that you, Andrew, tend to exaggerate your sphere of influence. Once you have an accurate picture of what you can control and what you cannot, then there's no room for anxiety or worry. You do all you can from sunrise to sunset to push on the boundaries of your influence. Work hard, work smart, think big, tend the garden of your friendships and relationships, live a moral & values-driven life to the fullest extent possible. If you do this, there is no room to worry that you're not doing enough. And, since that which is uncontrollable for me is, by definition, outside my sphere of influence, then there is nothing I can do there to change anything and therefore worry is for nothing.

So, stop worrying!

****

Perpetual Change

Ofri Hirsch, Soul Kitchen Chef
Born 1975. Afula, Israel

Ofri was born and raised on a kibbutz in Israel. Currently residing in Asheville, NC. She holds a Ba. Sc. from RMIT in Melbourne Australia and a MA in Urban Design from Harvard Graduate School of Design. She owns Asheville Mountain Kitchen designed to facilitate creative team building events. She also facilitates team building events online.

I was born and raised in Israel on a kibbutz (group) in Israel. A kibbutz is a revolutionary idea of a voluntary society in which people live in accordance with a specific social contract, based on egalitarian and communal principles in a social and economic framework.

Taking charge of my faith: Early years

While I have many great memories of boundless freedom from my childhood, I also remember the first attempt to break the group's strict rules. My first non-conformist moment was when I was 2.5 years old. At the time, the kibbutz kids slept communally overnight, away from the parents. We would be put to bed around 8 p.m., the parents then left us and we were supervised by an adult that was present nearby and could be reached by an intercom. This situation was not to my liking. I took matters to my own hands, placed a chair by a low window and jumped out into the dark night. I sneaked through the dark streets trying to avoid adults from seeing me, making my way to my parents' house. This act repeated itself until my parents took me in for good. My father later told me that I chose the darkest routes, running through the industrial zone for fear of getting caught. There was much resistance in the community but I won. I was the only child allowed to do so.

I was either stupid or brave but that was a good indication of what's to come.

Similar small battles were won by me during my kibbutz childhood; I refused to wear the group's identical hand-made clothes, refusal to work in child care like all the other girls, enough to assert my individuality but not too much to be expelled from the community or shun upon.

When I entered puberty, it was time to make "the big" move. I started feeling closed in. Questions were arising within myself, I wondered what else was out there, I was curious. I wanted to find who I was away from the group; I didn't want my life to be dictated by someone else. I was driven by curiosity and a feeling of independence.

Young adult: Early signs of explorations

The kibbutz I grew up in was located in northern Israel, in a lush area full of natural springs and mountains. I loved the natural environment around me and acquired great knowledge of the local flora and fauna. My love of the environment led me to a private boarding school that focused on environmental studies and science and was located in the south of Israel, an area called the Negev desert. The 3 years I spent there were eye opening. The students came from different backgrounds and regions, some have lived overseas, and it was a big change from the homogenous kibbutz environment. The boarding school provided me with a fertile ground to sow my seeds and pursue independent ecological research projects that have later led me to study landscape architecture.

Reflecting back, the thread that weaves the events in my life is driven by curiosity. I never let the setting restrict me. During my compulsory military service, I worked as an outdoors teacher, leading school groups through the dessert, camping and learning about the dessert environment. It was a very fulfilling occupation. Working with the groups I noticed that certain kids stood out from the crowd in their enthusiasm and curiosity. Even though it wasn't included in my job description, I started assembling those teens and created a special adventure group that would meet monthly to engage in special hikes to remote regions as well partake in nature conservation efforts. I still cherish those times, the friendships that were made, the innocence of youth with the backdrop of a beautiful virgin dessert scape. It shaped me as much as it shaped them. Growing up as part of a group and later in life leading the groups and teaching made me feel comfortable working with groups as a facilitator.

When I finished my service, my family had decided to move to Australia for my father's work. I was excited to join them as I was ready for a new adventure.

Immigration and Self-exploration

Anyone immigrating to another country entirely shakes the ground you stood on. It makes you question everything you know, especially at a young age. It also gives an outsider's perspective; I became a bystander. I enrolled in an undergraduate degree B.A. science in landscape architecture. Studying the urban environment combined by my observations of the new culture I was immersing in made me ask questions about the effect of our built environment on the culture and everyday interactions between people. I explored my interest by getting to know suburban Australia, I collected data on some of the common elements that make up the built environment, deconstructing those elements allowed me to re-assemble them to create a new model, speculating how it may affect overall culture and interactions.

Later on, I wanted to continue my studies, I was interested in the potential of taking a city based on urban sprawl such as Melbourne, Australia and turn it into a walkable city where people can manage without a car. When I mentioned the idea to my professors, they ridiculed me and asked, what is the point of that? Nobody will give up their car.

Once again I was getting a feeling that I need to broaden my horizons

My watershed moment was when I applied to the Harvard Graduate School of Design and got accepted. A chance encounter with an American developer landed me a scholarship.

My life took a sharp turn then. I liked the feeling of starting over, despite how overwhelming it felt at times. A fresh start releases the mind from conventions and connects yourself to who you really are. It unveils the layers around us and exposes our core values.

Looking back at my choices are made by finding the balance between Aspirations and emotions, as well as a more calculated consideration. I am a fairly balanced person in that regard. I don't just get swept away but I believe taking calculated risks can open up opportunities.

Since I was 16, I was battling an auto immune disorder. It has affected my life in many ways, good and bad. It is no doubt very limiting; Limited energy, dealing with pain and sometimes having to be dependent. It has also been very eye opening; it has shown who the people in my life that really care are. It developed a system of efficiency within me, in order to get my work done and leave time to rest. It taught me to take care of myself. Part of this condition has affected my child bearing and resulted in many miscarriages. One of those times was when I was 32 weeks pregnant, I had to undergo a late tern abortion. It required travelling to CO to a designated facility. I was doing it for medical reasons but everyone else that week was doing it for other reasons. While I couldn't know the full circumstances that has brought them to go ahead with such an extreme choice, It opened my eyes to "pro-choice" vs. "pro-life" debate and changed me forever in that regard. It showed me that our control is limited and life isn't worth living without creating and sharing my knowledge with people.

I am still exploring. I hope to create work that is fulfilling and can be done at an older age. During the past year my challenge has been balancing my work with family life, being focused and efficient amidst the chaos of the pandemic.

WHY do you aspire to live?
To make positive change, keep exploring.

WHO do you feel you are as a human being?
Mom, forever explorer.

WHERE do you think you are in your life?
I am in a relatively static state due to my young son. I am looking to change that in the near future and resume exploration.

WHERE do you think you will be when it ends?
Hopefully peaceful, fulfilled.

WHAT would you change to fully align your aspirations, emotions, thoughts and action?
Create more focus and clarity about how to move forward. Get out of my comfort zone, again!

To my younger self
Believe in yourself more, be less shy, more confident and go for what you want.

****

Designing with a Purpose

Doug Dietz, Innovative Design Thinker (see GE MRI machine for children)
Born February 4, 1958. Syracuse, NY, USA

Doug is currently Lead Innovation Architect for two key GE design incubators: GE Menlo Innovation Lab. He facilitates creative workshops (design thinking), immersing GE staff in a co-collaboration experience with customers. Adventure Series: Doug also is lead designer for the Adventure Series pediatric offering for patient experience. Crafting experiences to help families get through their healthcare journey while helping reduce patient sedation, increase patient throughput and increase patient satisfaction. Doug is an instructor at Stanford University for executive education d.school innovation courses. Doug's TED talk on 'Designing with a Purpose', https://www.youtube.com/watch?v=jajduxPD6H4.

My journey so far
Super lucky… I had a great family life growing up in northern Indiana. We had a large family and tons of kids in our immediate rural neighborhood to bond with in creative Play. Play has been a key influencer in my life. Learning to work together to bring the best out of each other has been the hallmark thread in my life. Neighborhood kinships, camp counselor leadership, sports enthusiast, and Family man with 3 children.

I was lucky enough to play ice hockey at Purdue University. This experience showed me the key cornerstones of "cultivating team genius" and allowed me to take on numerous rolls as player coach in many of my corporate assignments.

Directly out of graduate school, at the University of Illinois, I starting my career in Industrial Design at Texas instruments. My tenure in Dallas was highlighted by creating educational toys for kids to help them discover and learn as they played. My experience at TI also exposed me to the power of co-collaboration with our end-user and customers. My Human-Centered design skills were developed in my 7 years in the Corporate Design Center as part of the Innovation team.

I love the healthcare space and early on in high school I was strongly considering going into medicine. I visited my older sister, Carol, in Veterinary school and after turning blue during a tour of the surgery lab I knew I had to pursue a different route. When a position at GE Healthcare came across my path, I jumped on it. I spent 30 years working on all kinds of state-of-the-art diagnostic imaging equipment. Every time I got a little restless a new creative opportunity opened up. My last 10 years at GE I was asked to establish "incubator" projects that looked at healthcare outside our usual channels. This effort as Principal Designer was highlighted by my work on Adventure Series pediatric offerings and setting up and facilitating Design Thinking workshops with internal staff and Customers.

My watershed moment,
was in working with families in the pediatric radiology departments at Children's hospitals. I was amazed to realize that they had to sedate 80% of the children in order to have them hold still for their radiology exam. Learning the kids were just terrified of our large radiology equipment (MRI, CT, X-ray, Nuclear-Medicine) was humbling. We got to work and created an awesome experience that allowed the child to be the protagonist in a Hero's Journey. A swashbuckler on a pirate ship adventure, an Astronaut on an MRI spaceship, a voyager on a Jungle Adventure. The kids were allowed to imagine their own creative space much like "3 kitchen chairs and a blanket." Their creative spirit was given the green light to shape a personalized experience to make them comfortable. Sedation rates have plummeted, patient backlogs have decreased, department productivity is up, and the patient satisfaction rates have skyrocketed.

However, the pay-off for me was hearing a child ask "Can we come back tomorrow."

Personal challenge
A huge challenge for me was about halfway through developing the Adventure Series Pediatric offering I had a major healthcare scare. On a flight back from a business trip to France I felt strange and on the first night home I woke up feeling super weird. My left hand wasn't working and I couldn't speak. My wife, who is a nurse, realized what was happening and rushed me to the hospital. I had a stroke during the night. What a traumatic reset moment in life! I had to learn to tie my shoes, brush my teeth, and get dressed by myself. Another struggle was speech. Everything came out slurred. Through some great care at the hospital and tremendous support from my family I came through the struggle stronger. This personal experience with the "Patient's point of View" changed how I approached healthcare design. It gave me the courage to push the Pediatric Adventure Series through even when the business was not totally behind the effort. This experience also gave me the strength to bring a HCD/ Human Centered Design philosophy to our Global design organization. I created our Menlo-Design Thinking initiative to bring teams through immersive learning workshops to help them connect with the empathy of their end-users as well as move their challenges forward. This healthcare scare made me a much better designer.

Choice considerations
My choices in my design career have been influenced by empathy and truly understanding end-user's unmet needs and desires. Finding a problem worth solving and co-collaborating with customers has reshaped my thinking. Early in my career I thought I had to be the expert and have all the answers. I now understand that using the Human Centered Design process exposes awesome opportunities to make this world a better place.

The Pediatric Adventure Series really showed me that we don't have to submit to things not changing. Healthcare has been a pretty frustrating experience for many and it is truly terrifying for children... I learned it doesn't have to be that way. Amazing your customers can have terrific business results. Customers do determine your success.

WHY do you aspire to live?
Helping people find their creative spirit and give them permission to explore new frontiers.

WHO do you feel you are as a human being?
I define myself as someone who is a humble learner that wants to push past incremental change to make the world a better place.

WHERE do you think you are/will be in your life?
I think I am in a place in my life where I consistently get better every day and want to bring others along with me. I am not sure where I will be when it ends, but I know it will be remarkably different from where I am now.

WHAT would you like to change?
Change is good. If we keep doing things the same way and expecting different results, we know that is the definition of insanity, but we continue to do it all the time. So, I embrace change with open arms. I would like to work with teams that have a gnarly challenge and want to explore different ways of thinking, behaving, and influencing a cultural change in their organization.

Dimensional ratings
I think when you have a compassionate, humble nature and truly listen to your customers to learn not sell it will drive results. "Purpose for Power" can be a very selfish outlook and will not encourage many followers.

An advice to my younger self
'If you are not having fun it is ½ your fault'.

****

Following Faith

Yunsun Chung, Primary investigator for "Designing Food Revolution for Social Change"
Born 1964. Seoul, South Korea

I'm a designer, educator, researcher, and community builder. My passion is to contribute to youth empowerment and community engagement through co-design. I have planned and facilitated several empathy-driven, design-thinking workshops with youth since 2009 both locally in the UAE and internationally. Initiatives I have involved include KULNA (a research project that explores ways to co-designing food systems for social change); INNOCO (a co-designed community initiative to build social innovation); GYEM (a global youth empowerment), and tasmena (NGO design association). Currently, I'm the primary investigator for "Designing Food

Revolution for Social Change" action research while teaching graphic design at Zayed University, Dubai, UAE.

A few things came to mind when I think about my journey thus far—a blessing in disguise, crises and victories, and a commonality flowing through of a hero's journey as in everyone is walking through life with dignity and respect. I have a few watershed moments; when my beloved church members were disunited and disconnected from the church and fellowship; when I lost my dad with merciless cancers; when I was expelled from the Christian seminary and close Christian brothers and sisters become strangers over night for my investigations of truth were not accepted by the man-made creeds; when my husbands and 2 daughters were rejected by the parents in-law just because we became Baha'is and realizing that I don't have capacities to communicate my love and intention. I believe that my choices of what I want and should be done have been motivated by mostly aspirations. Many philosophers, thought leaders, and activists influenced my thoughts and values. My inclination towards respecting emotions also played a role to make decisions as believing that intuitive emotions are a guiding light reflecting divine attributes.

A series of events to shape my beliefs
As a granddaughter of an independent activist who gave his life to the nation, I have grown up with such a strong love for the nation. Family background and upbringing was deeply rooted in heroic and savior mentality. As a Korean born in a patriotic family whose members consist of an independent activist, Confucius follower, nature lover, Christian heretic, and many ambitious changemakers. Having philosophical visions and world views towards the common good was a very influential aspiration from a young age. Having a strong patriotic mentality to serve the nation was conflicted by the Christian commencement of 'love your neighbor." My inner conflict between a divine teaching that we must love thy neighbor and culturally fabricated love for the nation has resolved and a decision-making matrix has been shifted when I read a writing by Baha'u'llah: "Blessed and happy is he that ariseth to promote the best interests of the peoples and kindreds of the earth. It is not for him to pride himself who loveth his own country, but rather for him who loveth the whole world. The earth is but one country, and mankind its citizens." It opened my eyes to realize that loving your own county would not make sense as it caused so much problems such as wars and discrimination. Also,

it was a glimpse of hope that religious dogmas and narrow-minded understanding of what Creator for the entitled human race has bestowed His love and mercy.

WHY do you aspire to live?
My purpose to live is to grow my spiritual capacities as all humans have been created to carry forward an ever-advancing civilization. As a spiritual being, we all are experiencing a human life in such a short amount of time. As this world is a temporary place in a cosmic timeline and space in which we all continue to evolve as spiritual beings. Through this evolution, we all get to develop a relationship with the Creator and serve others while contributing to the betterment of the world. And I feel that this world is passing like a blink of an eye with a strong urgency. Hence a reason for being in this world is to know and to practice the truth. I'm a dedicated mother, passionate educator, enthusiastic community builder, lover of truth, and friend to whom I acquainted already and will be soon. "Be anxiously concerned with the needs of the age we live in, and center your deliberations on its exigencies and requirements." said by Bahaullah became my guiding light to prioritize what I need to be doing in this world.

WHO do you feel you are as a human being?
I'm a noble creature created by the Creator who created all human beings with the same. I know for sure that at the end of life, any title, any accomplishments, any material convenience and things will not help me to achieve a lifetime goal of being happy, contributing to peace and tranquility of the world. As a mother, wife, daughter, and friend to many beautiful fellow human beings, I feel privileged to be loved by family and friends, and desire to help others' life journey to be meaningful and somewhat easier by sharing what I know and shaping what I can do as a member of this planet. I strive to practice to see the rest of humanity as my fellow human beings who may cross my path. Though my passport identifies me as a Korean, at the core I'm a global citizen knowing these material systems in the world are progressively being developed towards oneness of humanity. Through this COVID pandemic time, we can't go back to the precious conditions without learning a lesson from high price paid challenges: "everything is connected and we must seek out collective solutions for everyone to live on this planet with harmony and justice."

WHERE do you think you are/will be in your life?
I have been saying that my lifetime goal is to be a cool grandma. I'm in a harvesting season with a basketful of stories; many prototypes attempted to bring meaningful social change from home, classrooms, and communities. Thus far, I acknowledged that whatever I tried to help others actually helped my spiritual capacities to grow. With actions, reflections, more questions and confirmation, I'm willing to continue my journey with fresh energy as if it just started. I have been given so much love, care, access to knowledge and amazing people and their projects. I'm standing at a place where I want to give more, want to be available when people need my help, and want to share my perspectives of what this earthly life is about. I don't know much about when it ends, but I know this life on earth is a mere opportunity to grow my spiritual capacities acquiring more virtues which might contribute to the betterment of the world.

WHAT would you like to change?
When aspirations, emotions, thoughts, and actions are aligned, we feel strong and happy. Though I strive to be more truthful and be of service to others, I find my shortcomings to a degree and intensity of the alignments. I believe that we can only keep trying. Consider any previous actions as prototypes and learn through reflections, then try again everyday towards more cohesive and impactful life. A few things I would like to change. (1) Any misaligned thoughts and actions by trusting the divine intervention at every moment like breathing, not occasionally. (2) My professional capacities from a professor to a learner by seeking and practicing a new educational paradigm, as a potential grass-root initiative. (3) My availability for others meant that I desire to spend more time and energy helping others instead of working on my urgent projects always. (4) Shifting priorities. Serving the community is not an extra thing anymore. Rather this is a higher priority as it is about people, souls, and global mindset shifts starting from my neighbor. For example, my husband and I started a biweekly interfaith devotional gathering with neighbors which expanded to more wider communities during Covid where friends are learning from each other's spiritual practices. It's a small microcosm where we committed to see more sameness than otherness.

Dimensional ratings
Aspiration can be a starting point it seems. It can guide and move emotions, thoughts and behaviors eventually. Life philosophies are guiding lights which are not linear rather integrative and holistic. Strong

purpose activates dormant compassion for change which creates a space to investigate thoughts/virtues of honesty for humility. Then all three can assist progressive behavior development which influences and determines the impact we want to see. And these transformative behaviors also allow access to deepen aspirations and perpetuates a progressive evolution growth. Also, aspirations can determine the quality and scopes of thoughts which can be driven by virtues of honesty for humility and provides opportunities to let go of EGO (dying and reborn). Ultimately this individual transformation process can contribute to the betterment of society by influencing positive behavior changes for societal transformation.

I truly believe that humanity is going through a major shift of rebuilding civilization in this age. As much as it's an ordeal to face climate changes and COVID pandemic scenarios, it's a wake-up call for all global citizens to realize that we are one human race and one human family. It's time to take our space from man-made decrees, regulations, and narrow-perspectives that disconnect us from nature (divine), people (society), and spirituality (self). And start helping each other to join force towards a new way of thinking and practices that will bring security and peace to the planet.

An advice to my younger self

You are on the right track. Keep up meaningful actions and reflections to increase your capacities to be more joyful and radiant, and be generous with your energy, time, and love with others.

****

Purpose Pursuit

Jaha Cummings, Councilman for the City of Punta Gorda, US
Born 1973. Coral Gables, FL, USA

Jaha grew up in Florida and graduated from Dartmouth College. After graduation, he moved to Tokyo, and lived and worked throughout Asia for 20 years. He specialized in market entry for healthcare companies and improving healthcare delivery in small countries. He also worked as a consultant in International Business Development and Cross-Cultural Communications. In Tokyo, Jaha founded a thinktank with a focus on youth and values formation and was a delegate to the G8 Summit in Japan. This evolved into a publishing house that now specializes in creating works for film, TV, game, and AR/VR adaptation. He is a member of Book Adaptation Rights Market of the Venice Production Bridge at the Venice International Film Festival. Jaha is co-founder of the Håya Foundation, an organization created to facilitate the revitalization of traditional Chamorro culture. Jaha is a Councilman for the City of Punta Gorda, serves on numerous Governmental and Non-Profit Boards, and is a member of Leadership Florida.

From the time that I can remember, I was taught by my family that we live to serve our purpose. Additionally, I was taught, to whom much is given, much is required. These are the principles that guided me through childhood into adulthood. As such, the decisions that I made as a child were those which were to enhance my ability to be able to serve my purpose. From around seven years old, I wanted to be a surgeon, so I had a very science-laden childhood, attending enrichment classes every summer at the university from the age of six culminating in a special graduate-level governor's program at the medical school and college of arts and sciences in biochemistry and cytogenetics. Throughout my childhood, I had always been very interested in learning about different cultures and perspectives of the world. During high school I co-hosted a television show which discussed historical and modern African and African-American contributions to the world. Out of this appreciation that I had developed about my culture, it caused an even greater appreciation within me for other cultures. I began doing consulting work in community development at age sixteen, facilitating workshops with my mother and on my own with community organizations in Florida and Connecticut. The basis of my work was in the development of healthy cultural esteem and its role in values formation and positive decision-making.

WHY are you here?
Despite having cultivated a strong background in the sciences up until the point of entering college, I came to realize that my first passion is culture.

WHO are you?
I derive from West African, English, Scottish, and Cherokee ancestry; and my family has maintained cultural practices from each of these groups. Being that I did not have Asian ancestry, I decided to study Asian languages cultures and languages. I decided to study Japanese first, because in doing so I would be semi-literate in Chinese because of a shared writing system. Having lived in Japan with a Japanese family in a homestay my sophomore year, I came to realize that I wanted to live in Japan. I felt that Japan was an environment that I could develop and express my creative potential. Throughout the remainder of my time in college, I worked towards this goal of living in Japan.

One of the main reasons that Japan was intriguing to me was because of how modern Japan was created. It was created through imagination. A national mythology was created by intellectuals and this national myth was the point of reference through which they industrialized. Japan matched the industrial production of Europe within a 40-year span. It can be argued that before the creation of modern Japan in the late 1800s, that there had not been a shared Japanese identity; rather, where one instead defined themself in relation to a feudal lord. Japan having created a nation through mythology and storytelling, illustrated to me how important the stories that we consume about ourselves and others are to the creation of ourselves and the world around us.

As I have mentioned, I have always seen my purpose as that of a healer
From early childhood, I wanted to be a doctor. I wanted to be an oncology surgeon; yet I was also very attracted to psychology, in particular, cognitive-behavioral therapy. My mother's doctorate is in counseling; and she has a particular expertise in cognitive-behavioral therapy, so as a child, I read many of her psychology books. The concept of cognitive dissonance always stood out to me. As a teenager, I was able to see her utilize this as a tool to improve the cultures of organizations in relation to how they treated their clients and each other. In short, cognitive dissonance is a psychological conflict where one has the self-realization that a belief that one has held about oneself is not true. In Cognitive-Behavioral Therapy, cognitive dissonance can be used to help people recognize erroneous and self-defeating thoughts and behaviors and change these in order to improve their lives.

For almost 20 years, I worked as a healthcare consultant. I assisted international medical device and pharmaceutical companies enter new markets; and I assisted small countries in developing their national healthcare delivery systems, particularly in radiology, orthopedics, laboratory, environmental health, and infection control/pandemic prevention. During this time, I also formally studied traditional African counseling and psychotherapeutic techniques. These healing modalities make extensive use of mythology and storytelling as psychotherapy. The goal of these sessions is to assist the client in coming into a state of congruence between their "head" and their "heart." In this state, one can more easily live their purpose and fully express their creative potential. To maintain this state, one's thoughts and actions need to be those that affirm positive relationships within oneself, with others, and with the natural environment.

WHERE do you stand in life?
A few years ago, I returned home to assist in local affairs. I was asked to run for local office and now serve as a city councilman. In this role, I serve on several city, county, regional, and statewide organizations. I see my purpose in this role is to eliminate barriers to and create the conditions that allow individuals, families, and communities to be able to reach their full creative potential. I find that I am most effective when I create shared understanding through storytelling. It is our imagination that liberates us to our true greatness or condemns us to being a foregone conclusion. It is through visualizing our lives as we wish to see them that we make the appropriate choices to bring these visions into manifest reality.

What is interesting about the city where I live is that it embodied this wealth of imagination in its inception. It is a pioneer town built from the efforts of a diverse group of people whose goal was to create a robust and mutually prosperous community. In its early days, it facilitated so much trade and embodied the best of Old Florida, Gulf Coast living, and seasonal tourism, that it was called the Grande Belle of Florida, one of the two most prosperous cities in the state. An interesting irony is that Punta Gorda, a small Southern city established after Reconstruction at the height of Jim Crow, was incorporated by both European and African-Americans. Its African-American Postmaster was a former State Legislator who is responsible for making free public education for all children in Florida. One of its other African-American residents who created one of the largest shipyards in Southwest Florida became one of the city's wealthiest men and largest landowners. His business was one of the first equal opportunity employers in the state of Florida; and kept people employed during the time when the rest of the country was experiencing the Great Depression. The point of me sharing this, is that if the residents of this town did not utilize their power of imagination and envision a world better than imagined in many other places around the country; and had maintained the social controls against African-Americans practiced in many places in both the North and South, the residents of the city would not have had a buffer against the poverty and hardship that many other Americans experienced during the Great Depression. During the first two decades of the twentieth century in the United States there are many cases of highly prosperous African-American business centers and communities destroyed through terrorism; to include those in Tulsa, Oklahoma; Ocoee, Florida; Rosewood, Florida; and Wilmington, North Carolina.

We are a collection of strengths
Together we mitigate each other's weaknesses and have collective access to "superpowers" whenever they are needed. There is an African proverb: "the slowest gazelle must be faster than the fastest lion." As such, it is through our combined strengths that we can overcome any adversity. Our goal is to become that bundle of sticks that cannot be broken. Therefore, we must encourage each other to be our own personal best. When one feels the radiance that they emit when they are expressing their true selves, one cannot help but desire to see this in others. It is this shared desire to shine brightly and bask in the light of others that we create community. This community, when built with the intention to be a place that nurtures the growth and full creative expression of its members, can withstand any challenge; and when faced with challenges, only becomes better because additional "superpowers" are revealed from within its members.

WHAT would you like to change?
I have found that the overarching goal of my life is to unify all the aspects of myself into a life that honors the diversity within myself and allows me to live in the most joyful fashion; one in which I am inspired to create joy and serve as an example of joy for others.

An advice to my younger self
We are all here to assist each other to fully express our light and to reach our destinies as fully manifest beings who live in a manner that

is welcoming to the future generations that come after us. We are here to reflect our light off each other, creating a mirror image of the Sun.

****

Note

1. This is but a small selection from a large and growing tribe of thinkers and doers who believe that change can and must happen, and who have begun to prove it through their own being and behavior.

CHAPTER 3

Shifting Focus: Zooming In and Out—My Story

Abstract Building onto the previous chapters this one offers additional angles to analyze an individual's life journey. The author's experiences illustrate how various prisms can be applied. The story-excerpts show how the complementary perspective of various entry points within one stream of experience can serve to explore blind spots and selective memory. Among these analytical prisms are the twice 4 dimensions of the POZE paradigm and the clusters of experience (people, places, privileges, problems); their respective usage is illustrated with examples.

Keywords Meaning · Potential · Alignment · Purpose · Compassion · Gratitude

From the time when I was a young girl, I trusted that my WHY was to make the World happier. Thus, I became an actor to show people how the World could be. Until I learned that the illusion of a changed reality does not change people's behavior. I then studied law to work on influencing legal systems, and attempt to obtain justice for those who cannot fend for their own needs. Until I realized that laws are worth only as much as the willingness of those who are meant to apply and enforce them. I thus became a humanitarian worker to help people affected by war, poverty, and disasters. Until I understood that we can bring others only

C. C. Walther, *Leadership for Social Change and Development*,
https://doi.org/10.1007/978-3-030-76225-4_3

what we have found inside. Unless our believes and behavior are aligned, our hands and heart remain empty. I was so focused on WHAT I wanted to be outside, my role in society, that I neglected WHERE I had to be within myself. One day a friend made me see what others had perceived all along: "Your purpose is to help others find theirs." Thus, I realized that the WHY of life means to unveil WHO we are, without veil nor veneer. Sharing outside WHO we are inside is our unique gift to this World.

Over the past 4 decades I had the opportunity to discover life from multiple angles. I have lived on a minimum and in prosperity. I nearly died 4 times and enjoyed extended periods of robust health. The so-called developed countries have been my home, as much as those that are supposedly underdeveloped. In both I found the prevailing stereotypes to be lacking truthfulness. I lived most of my life alone without being lonely, and found companionship in times when billions suffered from isolation. I have been immensely lucky throughout.

Becoming myself got easier when I acknowledged WHO I am (not). Accepting the point of departure (WHO I am now) whilst envisioning a goal (WHO I aspire to be) I began to change. To pursue the purpose that I have identified as mine, whilst remaining compassionate towards myself and others along the path, and honest about who I am (not) is not always easy; but continually worth it. It gets easier with awareness of the 4 dimensions that make us WHO we are—our aspirations, emotions, thoughts, and behavior. Consciously acknowledging and nurturing the ongoing interaction between my soul, heart, mind, and body helped to smoothen my interactions with others, because I became more centered and aligned within.

In the quest for inner optimization, I went through a transition within each of the 4 dimensions. Physiologically, I went from an omnivore diet to vegetarian to vegan. Intellectually, I moved from thinking to writing to teaching. Emotionally, I shifted from saving to possessing to sharing. Aspirationally, I travelled from wanting to finding to being.

Life is a classroom, in which we learn to grow. Looking back, 4 **formative clusters** emerge that marked me—places, people, privileges, and problems; a word on each:

Places (*Locations that left a mark*)—I grew up and studied in Europe, blessed by the fortune of a middle-class family that could afford to feed, educate, and protect me in a safe place. I worked in Africa, Asia, and the Caribbean, diving into cultures that were different from my own, to find the beautiful and sad, painful, and inspiring reality that evolves behind the smoke screen built by international media. I worked and lived in the US, discovering that I actually enjoyed the buzz of a megapolis like New York; and the luxury of amenities such as running water and unhindered electricity. I returned temporarily to Germany to support my parents during a dark period. Whilst COVID was strangling the world in its second wave, my father was approaching the end. Both dynamics reminding me of the inherent limitations of life.

People (*Thinking of them as teachers, whether they nurtured, challenged or denigrated us*)—People enter our life to help or teach us a lesson, to convey a message, or to accompany us during a part of our journey; some come to stay. I have been very lucky with those who came, both those who remained and those who left. My preference of being alone rather than in bad company served me well. There is no place as lonely as the space we share with someone who does not care for nor share your perspective; or has no desire to understand it.

Other than my parents, whose behavior and personal inclinations naturally influenced me, 4 individuals come to mind when I seek to identify one person who influenced me in each dimension. *Soul*—my first boss taught me that it is possible to live your life without compromise; to accomplish challenging work that has the potential to improve the lives of others—those under his supervision, and those targeted by his professional scope; all of this while thoroughly enjoying the ride because your aspirations are aligned with your actions, and you leave dedicated space for the loved ones that matter to you. *Heart*—a woman, who took me in while I was studying in France, showed me that love is giving. Trusting the farmer (another person of the heart) whose longtime customer she was, and who I was working for to fund my living expenses, she offered me free lodging in her home, a beautiful old palace in the heart of the city. The traumatic events of her life had not tarnished but kindled her kindness. Losing her husband to suicide and her daughter to cancer, a disease she was battling for decades and ultimately succumbed to, did not push her to focus on herself. Like a flower she was turning to the world and helped those around her. *Mind*—while the aforementioned individuals inspired me to follow their example, this one accomplished a precious part in my personal learning, by showing me how I did not want to be. Whilst working in Africa she was one of my supervisors; showing me first-hand certain behaviors that I myself had a tendency for (such as harsh discipline towards yourself and others, no matter the cost) and their disastrous impact on those in her environment. She also made me understand the crucial lesson that life is a mirror. We see in others what we like/dislike in ourselves. When it is a side that we shun in our own being it becomes a red button in the interaction with those who show that behavior. *Body*—a man who loves my soul and heart, my mind and body gave me the confidence to fully embrace my physical shell. The experience of being accepted unconditionally, from the inside out and vice versa gave me grounding at a time when everything was changing.

Privileges (*Assets, material and immaterial*)—I was born in Germany a safe country with a horrendous history, to parents that could offer me the resources I needed to thrive. Over the course of my career, I met countless girls and women who would never get an opportunity to reveal and develop their innate skills and resources; individuals who were more intelligent and talented than I am, yet who evolved in a context that was at best allowing them to survive, without nurturing their aspirations and abilities. Living this discrepancy between what is and what should be over the two decades of my work in the so-called developing countries, experiencing the obvious injustice that it portrays made me acutely aware of the giant lottery ticket that I had won without playing. It made me grateful for who I am and what I was given. But it also fed an inner void that has always been there, the need to try and change what feels wrong.

Problems (*Overcome and ongoing*)—Life is a journey, and the hardest hurdles are those of our own making. My path to liberation began from the inside out and was nurtured from the outside in. Releasing the need to shape and control the outside has set me free to attempt the becoming, inside, of my own best self. The gradual establishment of an honest relationship with myself was uncomfortable and at times unbearable, until it became light and soft like silk. The challenge is that once we own up to our reality, acknowledging who we truly are, and who we are not, there is no turning back. When everything crumbles there is nothing to turn to, nothing but ourselves. This perspective is frightening until we discover how welcoming the inner realm is.

Besides these 4 clusters—which you may distinguish in your own journey, life can be charted in various other ways:

- *The 4 questions that underpin our path—Why, Who, Where, What.*
- *The 4 dimensions—soul, heart, mind, body, or, aspirations, emotions, thoughts, sensations.*

- *The 4 arenas in which we spend our time and resources—growth, love, work, play.*
- *The 4 attitudes that influence our path– perspective, optimism, zeal, excellence.*

One word on the last group which is the only one that has not been explained in more detail so far—*Perspective* is influenced by the aspiration to purpose. It evolves as we do (Soul/WHY). *Optimism* is an emotional attitude that entails the ability of looking for the positive that does, could, or will derive from a situation. It is an attitude that can be consciously trained (Heart/WHO). *Zeal* relates to a mindset of commitment; of not giving in nor up, which influences where we end up in life (Mind/WHERE). *Excellence* does not relate to outputs, but to the attitude of giving our best in any situation, based on the values, knowledge, and skills that we have and care about at the time of action (Body/WHAT). Using any or all of the proposed angles to analyze your own journey you may notice their complementarity when it comes to identifying the blind spots of our memory. The individuals in Chapter 2, were explicitly asked the 4 macro-questions which relate to Purpose (WHY), Personality (WHO), Position (WHO), and Pro-activity (WHAT) as an illustration of the POZE paradigm which underpins this book. In answering them they explored the 4 dimensions (soul, heart, mind, and body) from which these questions derive as well as the 4 related arenas of energy investment (growth, love, work, play). From their reflections 4 attitude angles emerge (perspective, optimism, zeal, excellence) appeared.

To complete the illustrative storytelling in this chapter, I will in the following section use the 4 dimensions directly to look at my journey of becoming.

3.1 The 4 Dimensions

3.1.1 Body

Control amid uncertainty could have been the stated moto of my life until recently. Growing up, all indicators of child wellbeing were in the green zone; or so it seemed. Underneath the polished surface, the tectonic plates were shifting constantly. The omnipresent tension that seemed to underpin our family made the break-up an ever-lingering possibility. In addition, we were moving frequently, from one city to another, including new schools and unfamiliar people. The result was a layer-cake of uncertainty; that left my body as the only space under my control. In parallel to school, I undertook intensive ballet training; stopping only when it became a choice between full-time dance or university. As I entered the professional world, the tangible, material sphere once again was the anchor I held on to. A superficial feeling of safety came as my career flourished and my bank-account grew. Money and status gave me a sense of accomplishment; the impression that my life proceed within a riverbed that I had traced and had control over. Until I realized that I had mistaken as pillars of support what were stones that pulled me down. I had chained myself sub-consciously to people, places, power, and possessions; relinquishing the biggest asset of all, freedom. Once I began to connect the dots, the complementarity of those opposing needs—safety versus freedom emerged. Rather than mutually exclusive these needs were actually part of the same spectrum of my being. I had merely gravitated from one end to the other.

Releasing a perspective that seemed engraved in stone gives us access to its counterpart; which we may have longed for all along. Life changes, and so do we. Never standing still; neither our experiences, nor our thoughts or our emotions are immutable. So many factors, internally and outside, are at play within the constantly evolving kaleidoscope of our existence that the quest for control is futile.

I have long mistaken the material world as a platform to get a grip on reality, because it contains tangible factors that can be seen and touched. However, using it as a fence to trace "my" territory in delimitation from the rest, I had imprisoned rather than secured myself. Investing time and thought to acquire assets and accomplishments that ultimately held me back rather than setting me free. Allowing myself to let go what was gone I opened my hands to embrace new space.

3.1.2 Mind

I always needed to understand the World I operated in; never ready to settle for the answers I was given. Stuck in my mental space I started out to become an actor, *thinking* I would show people how the world could be, and thereby make them change their behavior to create that world off-stage. I learned that people do not change because of things they are told. I quit and studied law, *thinking* I could establish laws to protect those most at risk of marginalization, children, women, minorities—those who often lack the possibility to defend their needs. I learned that the Law is worth only as much as the willingness of those who are meant to implement and enforce it; which leaves a vast gap between legal theory and practice. Many years later my Ph.D. looked at the breach between rights and reality that children experienced in most countries that signed the Convention on the rights of the child (CRC). I confirmed that an individual and collective obligation precedes the legal setting; it derives from our human nature. (But confirming this fact in theory and on paper does not change the status quo from being what it is in practice).[1] I quit law and worked as a humanitarian worker with the United Nations, attempting for two decades to promote children's rights in Mali, Chad, Afghanistan, the Democratic Republic of Congo, and in Haiti. Over time I learned that many institutions whose vocation it is to make the world a better place remain underneath their potential. A central factor seemed to be the discrepancy between on the one hand the beautiful mandate and the inspiring values of these organizations, and on the other the attitude and action of certain staff members. Stereotypes do not apply and during my time on the frontlines I experienced the whole range of human behavior from courage, compassion, and creativity to hypocrisy and egocentrism. Though the drive for purpose and the urge to relieve suffering is strongly developed among many who choose the humanitarian sector as a line of work, human needs and desires are just as diversified here as they are in any other line of work.

Too long was I stuck in my mind. Hiding behind rationality, in the vain attempt for control. Mistaking connotations for meaning; intellect for impact; unravelling for untangling. Caught in a loop of questions and answers I built myself a fortress with thick walls to suffocate the silent cry for understanding not just others but myself.

3.1.3 Heart

When I was six years old my mother told me that she would leave my father. She asked if I was ready to come. I said no, she stayed. Over the following decades I witnessed the consequences of my re-action. There was no physical violence; but words of venom cut deep. As I was growing up my senses served to bear witness of how the person whom I cherished most in the world was denigrated. I did not do anything. Helpless, useless, a bystander to the injustice that took place in my immediate environment. That "no" spoken as a small child inflicted me with guilt on three levels: I *felt* guilty because I witnessed the insults, the shouting, the abuse without doing anything to protect my mother; I *felt* guilty because she would have escaped that situation had she not stayed, for me; and I *felt* guilty because I still wanted to please my father. Thus, my heart was split in two; with one side full of anger against him, and the other filled with love, longing to be loved in return.

Eventually I grew a shell to shield my softest core. I protected my Self from myself. Putting a blanket over the incoherence of my feelings, the guilt of being a coward, the guilt of longing for a love I felt was undeserved. I refused to accept these contradictory feelings as a natural manifestation of being human.

3.1.4 Soul

I craved *meaning* throughout my life. The urge to fill an emptiness that loomed inside. It is an instinctive drive that led me along a meandering path of becoming. I tried to give *meaning* to others, in the quest of finding it inside. A while back I took a sabbatical and began to write. Putting to paper POZE, the paradigm that the present publication is based on. Several books ensued. The point of departure was the conclusion of my Ph.D.—that an obligation is inherent to humanity which precedes the law** : **we must use our privileges to help those who lack them. Yet social change does not happen even when people must act; it does happen when they want to get involved. Lasting transformation occurs when we want to bring change, and when we are ready to change ourselves for starters.

As mentioned earlier POZE means inner peace in Haitian Creole, the country where I began to test and teach the paradigm and the related methodologies, which had been long in the making. Adolescents, social workers, UN staff; independently of age and background, religion, and culture—I found within all of them the same, often repressed, craving for meaning. We needed a reason, a WHY to be. That urge may be buried or out in the open, but it is always there; waiting to be addressed. The answers to that WHY are as diversified as our respective selves. There is, however, a common denominator that matters, the desire of reaching beyond ourselves to connect with others. When we connect and share with others in a meaningful manner, we bring meaning to our own life. The happiness of others and our own are complementary, one without the other is not sustainable. Thus, what we do for others we do for ourselves. Generosity towards others, is generosity for our selves.

The 4 dimensions can take us on a long journey. For decades I sought meaning in material, outward-oriented aspects. I failed to find meaning in matter, caught in a doomed quest to matter. Disregarding the core of meaning—the disinterested act. I craved to understand whilst closing my eyes from the feeling that was meant to set me free.

3.2 Lessons Learned

Looking at the end puts things into perspective.

I am standing here because I was lucky and want to give back. Four times since I was born, I received the gift of life because it was not taken from me.

The first time I was 12. Brought to the hospital for a simple stomach condition, one night my small intestines (which are supposed to turn smoothly) slung themselves into a knot. If an off-duty doctor had not come to my room to double check, following an inch of intuition, I would not be here.

The second time I was 22. After a year of relentless studying, I was turned down from the scholarship that would have allowed me to study abroad. I turned my disappointment into excessive sport. Going on vacation by myself I spent the days walking. From the first blink of sunlight until dark. Walking to numb the pain. At the end of the week, I was scheduled to meet my father in a nearby town. I walked there in the burning sun. Barely arrived, I collapsed. I am here because he called an ambulance on the spot. I was rehydrated (and accepted into the coveted study program the following year).

The third time I was 32 working with UNICEF in Afghanistan. One day I returned from a trip to Kandahar, and my plane was late. Upon arrival in Kabul, we were informed that the only road between the airport and the city was blocked because a car bomb had blown up five minutes earlier, killing three Italian soldiers. I was lucky because I was late.

The fourth time was the first time—I was lucky when I was born as a white girl, in a safe country to loving parents who were able to feed, protect, and care for me. From my first breath I have been lucky. And the feeling to feast from a lifelong jackpot made me grow up in the understanding that there is a direct correlation between privilege and responsibility. We can and must seize our assets and abilities to help those who were less lucky. Living up to our highest self, starts when we make the connection between what we have and what we give. Bridging the gap that separates those who have from those who are deprived is not an option. It is an obligation and a privilege of those who can to help those who need it. Without merit I escaped death repeatedly. Now I try to do something with the spare time that I was given; acutely aware that what we are and become is conditioned by circumstances and the people around us.

****

It is an old Buddhist saying that we need to prepare a good death in order to live a good life (Rinpoche 1992). "*Without our familiar props, we are faced with just ourselves, a person we do not know, an unnerving stranger with whom we have been living all the time but we never really wanted to meet. Isn't that why we have tried to fill every moment of time with noise and activity, however boring or trivial, to ensure that we are never left in silence with this stranger on our own?*" (Rinpoche 1992). It is a precious perspective to reframe our worries and wants, which does not need to be prompted by external events. We can choose to keep death, the counterpart of life which we all, without exception, encounter, present in our mind.

WHY we are in this World determines WHO we become in it—as a person, as member of a community, as citizen of a country, as a human being on Planet Earth. We are not only connected to our environment and those around us—we are a part of them. Constantly evolving as they do. When we consciously embrace this understanding, aware that we are part of an inter-connected continuum that constantly evolves—where starting and ending continuously complement each other—we *become change*.

Note

1. If you are interested to follow that train of thought, see Walther (2014).

References

Rinpoche, S. (1992). *The Tibetan Book of Living and Dying: The Spiritual Classic & International Bestseller: 25th Anniversary Edition*. ISBN: 9780062508348.

Walther, C. (2014). The Responsibility for Children's Rights. University of Law, UIII. Aix-en-Provence.

CHAPTER 4

Tools to Find Out More

Abstract This book is a point of departure. It is part of an organic dynamic to connect likeminded thinkers and doers, who aspire to change and be change. Everyone is welcomed. Anchored in the logic of the paradigm that underpins this book, the selected tools in this chapter may serve the reader in two ways to experience the presented theory in practice. It may, thus, on the one hand help those who have not found their purpose yet to get started; and on the other hand, support those who already found their passion to channel their energy into transformative action.

Keywords Mindset · Attitude · Perspective · Optimization · Zenith · Exposure · Tools

4.1 The Self-Equation and Deriving Tools to Explore It

Everything is connected.

Example—A situation occurs. It is experienced by the body via our sense tools. It is neutral, neither good nor bad. Then, depending on our past, the mind snaps into action, generating thoughts, which trigger emotions, pleasant or unpleasant. Judgements and qualifications of the situation

C. C. Walther, *Leadership for Social Change and Development*,
https://doi.org/10.1007/978-3-030-76225-4_4

arise, like or dislike. These emotions generate more thoughts, which eventually manifest in an expression, physical or vocal. This expression influences the situation, resulting in new experiences which are taken in via the senses, generating more thoughts and hereby emotions. It depends on our expressions whether these experiences confirm our existing beliefs and positions—which are the undercurrent of our present thinking, or if they change what we thought previously of as right/wrong. This circle perpetuates itself. It depends on our present action whether it is vicious or virtuous, in support of our aspirations or endangering their pursuit.

****

This link of past and future becomes a challenge when the *Evolving I* (Sect. 1.3.1) contains outdated left-overs that served as coping mechanisms in the past yet address threats that no longer exist. Letting go of these mechanisms may seem radical. After all, what remains when we are stripped of our shields and shells? Yet the question is not to relinquish everything that we have and cherish, just the attachment that binds us to them. When we dissolve the add-on that we hold towards them we liberate ourselves from them without having to give them up. When we release the craving towards the subjects and objects that matter to us, we can continue to experience them. Actually, we enjoy them more, because we experience them without distortion. Remember, there is no technique to surrender. You simply let go. The only way past is through.

4.1.1 Craving and Aversion

Emotions of joy, sadness, anger, fear, disgust, and love happen as a result of our circumstances. However, what ultimately triggers a (re)action in those circumstances is the experience of craving and aversion, desire and dislike that accompanies our emotions.

Depending on the proximity in which they are located to the core of our being our feelings manifest with varying degrees of intensity. The closer an issue is to what we cherish as our identity, the more painful the feelings that are triggered by it are to address; and the more forceful our re-action tends to be. The feelings that are most tender are the ones anchored in our soul, or our (sub)conscious quest of meaning.

Aspiration to meaning in the sense of a calling is a major factor of influence in our emotional environment. Around the world, disillusionment and a void of meaning causes depression, suicide, substance abuse and ultimately result in violence against ourselves or others. Conversely, the pursuit of a purpose, together with positive social relationships, was found to be the key of a healthy happy life.[1] Aspirations are not something that can be designed or adopted. They evolve as we live, and with them the deriving emotions. However, what we do, how and for whom we do it, influences directly and indirectly the course that this evolution takes.

The desire for change arises from the inside out, and it is nurtured from the outside in. Yet whatever influence we want to have on the core of our being (our aspirations and emotions) starts through the outer layers (our thoughts and behavior). Through conscious practice we can eventually strengthen the influence that we have over our thoughts and (re)actions, and hereby (in)directly influence our emotions and aspirations. Conversely, our aspirations and emotions directly influence our thinking and behavior, even the way in which we perceive and experience what happens around us. From moment to moment, we are thus subject to the impact of our present aspirations and emotions (*Experiencing I*) that are shaped by our past thoughts and behavior (*Evolving I*). It is a spiral dynamic that works both ways; and which can be influenced in our favor once we acknowledge and address the connection.

While we have no direct control over our emotions, our thoughts and hereby our behavior are subject to conscious influence. They offer doors to influence how we interact with ourselves and others; and hereby to influence our experiences and the underpinning and deriving emotions. The kind of internal dialogue that we entertain impacts how we perceive ourselves and the situation we are in. If the inner voice that is our constant companion is unkind and impolite it is possible to retrain it. Life brings enough external adversity, there is no need to entertain internal hardship beyond an absolute minimum.

4.1.1.1 Our Spiraling Being and Becoming

The next two sections cover similar ground as Chapter 1. By going deeper into what was described in a more abstract manner there, the aim here is to facilitate understanding via practical tools that are proposed for you to experience the relevance and benefits of the overall theory first-hand.

Our being is like a snail; the soft and vulnerable parts are located at the core, protected by a hard, resistant shell. External events come in contact with that shell—the body, which takes it in via the senses; these impressions are then distilled and digested by the mind which acts like a filter between the outside and the inside, tasked to identify potential danger. Like the mouth, throat and lungs are lined up to filter out impurities in the air, with increasing refinement as the air penetrates deeper into the body, protecting vital organs from polluting particles, the mind is designed to protect our heart and soul. Like the skin which has up to seven layers of ectodermal tissue, guarding the underlying muscles, bones and organs, whilst protecting the organism from dehydration. Each dimension (body, mind, and eventually the heart are protecting the soul) has a specific set of functions that is complementary to the others; all are geared to protecting what's underneath.

The mind treats incoming "information," decoding what comes up on the radar. Based on past experiences it offers interpretations and explanations. Our emotions are activated by the results of this process, which acts like an airbag. However, they may backfire at the wrong occasion. Because what we did in a past situation of a similar kind, and the result of that behavior, influence the course of action that we choose in the present. Since the mind draws on past experiences, the thought processes that it comes up with in a new situation are necessarily outdated. Our being has evolved in the meantime. Though we may now be aware that the course of action then was not ideal, or even harmful to us or others—we are prone to repeat this same behavior; like a truck that sees the bus but cannot stop brusquely from one moment to the next.

The challenge of this spiraling constellation, which is meant to protect us, is two-fold:

As we move through life our experiences accumulate, and with that the density of our mental filters increases. The child's mind has a basic setup coming from its genetics and other factors, but overall, it is pristine. Exposure to external inputs, including education and environment, gradually shapes how we perceive the world and interact with it. Every situation contributes to this stock of filters which are then deployed in subsequent situations. As we grow older it becomes ever rarer that an experience completely surprises us, throws us off track, immerses us in awe. Even if an unusual event occurs, the mind has a filter ready that somehow matches, at least partially, the situation at hand. Though in principle this is a beautiful and useful mechanism, which allows humans to function in society, it can have disastrous consequences. Because not all our past experiences and expressions were positive.

When our system was still young and soft, with the outer layers barely developed, the core was close to the surface. Dramatic events entered directly in the emotional sphere. In the absence of a mental buffer, they left deep marks. In parallel, repeated external influences of less intensity were gradually embedded into our mental makings, like drops of water that add up and eventually fill the cup to the rim. Though the mental shield grows thicker over time, whatever enters our path and how we react to it, leaves imprints for later. Every action that we take has influence. Directly because of the immediate impact of our action in our environment, and indirectly because how we think, feel and as a consequence of that, express ourselves—through verbal or physical action, results in an experience. This experience is taken in via the body's senses, digested in the mind based on past experiences of a similar type, and archived to be drawn upon in the future. The result of this process enters the emotional sphere which reacts to it, with liking or disliking. If the result of this three-step distillation (body, mind, heart) touches a soft spot in our soul, because it poses a threat to our identity and self-worth, aspirations kick-in as the last instance. Even a small action taken today may thus have far-reaching impact in the future; like a seed that is planted today may grow into a cactus or a mango tree; like a stone dropped into the water resulting in ever expanding ripples on the surface.

Sometimes the shell breaks and either light or darkness enter the vault of our soul. Certain events crush us, throw us off balance, chew us up, and spit us out; making any available reference point irrelevant. These can be opportunities, gifts in disguise to rise from pain like a flower through the ashes on burned ground.

The second challenge is that an overactive mind prevents us from direct contact with reality. Unless we gain control over it, the mind automatically snaps in, acting as an interface between the inside and the outside; allowing no raw immediate contact between the soft core and the outside. We are so busy thinking about the situation and how we should (not) react to it, that we have no free mental capacity to be present. Unless we re-train our mind to treat the incoming elements objectively, from scratch, we live in Plato's world of shadows, dealing with leftovers from the past. Based on outdated filters we are immersed in outdated thinking and derived from it, outdated feeling. Since we are not experiencing reality as it actually is, but how it appears to us through the filter-prisms, we do not even realize that we are out of synch; fighting shades on a screen, rather than facing the backstage where they come from. The behavior that eventually results from this inner process is, unsurprisingly, out of synch with reality too.

Nobody outside can save us. We seem captured in the mesh of our past, caught in the looping of past experiences and expressions, but we are not. We are stuck only until we move. Every moment offers an opportunity to consciously step out of the loop; until the mesh dissolves. Two concrete steps are required for this dissolution, awareness and proactive behavior. The benefits of this shift in attitude and action are immediate, with pay-offs in the medium- and long term. Let us look at both briefly, including tools to develop them.

4.1.2 Freedom and Awareness—Tools

In the context of Freedom, Awareness means two things. On the one hand we require *awareness of the interplay between mind and matter*, between our internal layers and our outside behavior. Because when we understand how we operate, we understand *why* we re-act in certain ways. Once we are familiar with the process underneath, we can begin to systematically influence both—the process and what results from it. Learning to consciously influence our inner dynamics means moving from being a bystander in life to a proactive stance in it. This is the origin of "empowerment."

The collateral benefit of this awareness to our inner interplay is that it offers insight into the operating systems of others. Because whether we want to influence what others do directly, or simply seek harmonious relationships, we must first understand why they are the way they are.

In the same way in which our past experiences and expressions shape our current behavior, and in which our prevailing aspirations, emotions, and thoughts influence our words and actions, those around us are shaped by their internal setup too. Understanding this is a powerful asset. It nurtures compassion, with ourselves and others. This nurtures our social relationships. We no longer just see but feel other perspectives, which shows up entry points on how to best convey our interests so that they are acknowledged and addressed by those whom we interact with.

On the other hand, we need *awareness of reality* as it is. Instead of facing a self-made screen we must experience what enters our path, without filters that distance our inner world from the fresh input of living. Though they may sometimes offer protection, overall, internal preconceptions prevent us from exploring the Now, which is the only place where change—of ourselves and the world—takes place. The shift from filters to facts begins with a conscious choice. Instead of spending our time and energy enmeshed in a web from the past, busily knitting one strand after the other, we can press pause. The bonus of this effort is actual exposure to the beauty of the present, the clean colorful direct experience of that which is, the ever-surprising sparkles that mark each moment.

The body is a tangible entry point to get started and be present (Tool-1, Tool-2).

> *TOOL-1* Physical experiences (such as touch, smell, sight, sound and taste) are neutral, until we put the stamp of judgement. Concentrating on the step between experience (neutral) and judgement (like/dislike) is a practical way to sharpen unbiased awareness of that which is. We can train ourselves to simply take in what happens, without verdict nor categorization.
>
> During your day you may wish to reserve a POZE-moment, to
> **P**ause (put down everything and lean back),
> **O**bserve (take in everything around you, seek to fully see, hear, smell, taste, touch your environment),
> **Z**oom inside (close your eyes and take the same neutral observation stance inside, noticing your thoughts and feelings without judgment or attachment), and
> **E**xperience (be in that moment, nothing more, nor less).

*

> *TOOL-2* Another way to enter the presence is a focus on the breath.
> Follow attentively your breath as it comes in, moving from the nostrils inside, upkeeping the circulation of oxygen that keeps you alive. Trail it until eventually it comes out, to dispose of the accumulated carbon dioxide that would harm your organism. This process conditions our survival. We are constantly engaged in it, and yet barely notice it until problems arise, i.e., asthma, cough, COVID-19. The breath is our constant companion, a loyal reminder of change and continuation; of complementarity (oxygen/carbon dioxide) and connection (in/out), of here and now.

Pursuing these practices on a regular basis strengthens our awareness acuity. The more we practice, the less energy it eventually takes us to maintain attention. Over time we can thus go deeper; gradually acquiring a feel of the environment as it actually is. Eventually, as our experience of the environment changes, our expressions in this environment change. Thus, our inner stock of memories is refreshed. The filters are cleaned, and gradually removed. From simple to complex our archive gets a makeover. Starting with straightforward impressions of the people and places around us, we move ever deeper inside, until we reach the embedded, sensitive parts of the past. Eventually letting go of those that no longer serve us (Tool-3).

*

> *TOOL-3* Think about a challenging experience. Distil in which sequence the 4 dimensions (sensations, emotions, thoughts, aspirations) came into play as you went through it. Look at each component objectively, without dislike or attachment. Then carefully choose which of your past patterns is worth keeping for your future.

When (mental) trash is deleted, space opens for fresh air, and new perspectives. Rooted in the aspirational core of our being, like violets obstructed by weed in an overgrown garden, our aspirations come to the surface. As light gets in, light shines out; manifesting as different behavior.

Eventually our core is renewed, finding its original purity. Though this is a long and laborious process, benefits come along the way, like fruits on trees that nourish wanderers as they explore an uncommon track. If we work persistently, we start to notice changes, in our day-to-day behavior. We become more patient and compassionate with ourselves and others. This process of transformation can be activated from the outside in—from behavior to thought to emotion to aspiration; and from the inside out—triggered from aspiration to emotion to thought to sensation (Sect. 1.3.1). Eventually a new, pulsating, stronger core substitutes the old one.

Understanding what (actually) *is* conditions our ability to create what *could* be.

Our aspirations and antipathies are a complex mix of thoughts and sensations, which is outside our immediate control. We can only influence how we react to them. Our best chance to escape what traps us is working on the aspects that are located within our reach, above and below the surface (Tool-4).

*

TOOL-4 A new dynamic can be nurtured through a simple 4-step sequence that links Acknowledgement, Awareness, Apprenticeship, and Action (delay & digest):

1. *Acknowledgement*—Take time to acknowledge the 4 dimensions of your being right now. [Ask yourself: What matters most to me, now and here. What do I believe in (Aspiration)? How am I feeling (Emotion)? What am I thinking, right now (Thought)? What is going on around me, what do I see, hear, feel, smell, touch (Sensation)?]
2. *Awareness*—Notice the interplay between these 4 components. [Ask yourself: How is what I think influencing how I feel and vice-versa? How are my desires influenced by what I think, what I feel? How are my wishes, emotions, and thoughts influencing my perception of the environment? How is what I see/hear/smell/taste/touch influencing what I want, feel, think and do?] Consciously distilling the sequence of physical input, mental interpretation, and emotional reaction is useful to understand how the spiral turns in both directions. <u>From the inside out</u>—Identify when and how your aspirations, your emotions, your thoughts are at (inter)play; which dimension is activated first? <u>From the outside in</u>—Notice how these inner dimensions are affected by sensorial triggers (sight, touch, smell, taste, sound; words and behaviors).
3. *Apprenticeship*—Train your awareness to notice the space between your experiences (sensations) and your expressions in re-action to these external triggers (behavior). With practice in this dimension-distillation you gradually learn to widen the space between intake and output. That inner space between sensorial triggers and re-action to them comes with the luxury to choose your action, rather than reacting as a result of semi-automatic impulses.
4. *Action*—There are two aspects of action: Delay and Digest—(Delay) Consciously delay the expressions that would have been triggered by the (outdated) automatisms that you have lived with so far. (This gradually leads to new behavior patterns that overwrite the existing ones.[2])(Digest)—Experience your environment, consciously removing your own filters [Ask yourself—How does what I want, feel and think right now influence the way in which I perceive this situation/this person? How do my past experiences influence my perception of this current moment]?

It is a choice to either ignore, or systematically work with the continuum of past, present, and future. Instead of repeating our acquired behavior/thought/emotion patterns, strengthening them whilst getting ever more entangled in them, we can consciously step out, ever and again, starting and nurturing a new cycle. Each situation that triggers a certain behavior pattern is an opportunity to start changing the past pattern, in line with our present-day aspirations. The deeper rooted the old pattern is, the harder it is to change it. But with each repetition this 4-step sequence gets easier. A new dynamic is set in motion.

In the wording of neuroscience—new neural pathways are created which overwrite the existing ones. (Doidge 2007). In the words of meditators—stored impurities from the past ("sankara" in the Pali language of Gautama the Buddha) come to the surface, and by acknowledging them without reacting, they pass away. It is our choice to be prisoners of our past, or leaders of our future (Fig. 4.1).

Tools to explore the WHY to influence the WHAT, and hereby the WHO and WHERE

Becoming WHO we aspire to be entails identifying what the best version of ourselves is. Once we have inner clarity it becomes possible to visualize what our *Being I* will look like in the future, whilst monitoring how the *Experiencing I* behaves in the presence.

The aim of such ongoing self-monitoring is two-fold. It serves us to:

1. *Keep track of our own attitude*, whether we remember and still care consciously about the issues that we had identified as essential for the overall evaluation of our life (i.e., you dreamt of being an activist to halt climate change, yet your life navigates around cash, career, cars, and casual sex).
2. *Adjust as needed when we notice lacking pursuit of our aspirations*. Because the latter can be due to either a dissonance between our objectives and our actual behavior (i.e., I want to write a book, but have not put one sentence to paper) or an alteration of those aspirations (i.e., I always wanted to work as a humanitarian worker on the frontlines to help those in need of life-saving assistance; then I settled down, got married, and had children; whereas my job was front and center, now the main focus has shifted towards my family. Work has become an activity that generates money and status, no passion). Either way, change is needed that requires choices that no one can take for us.

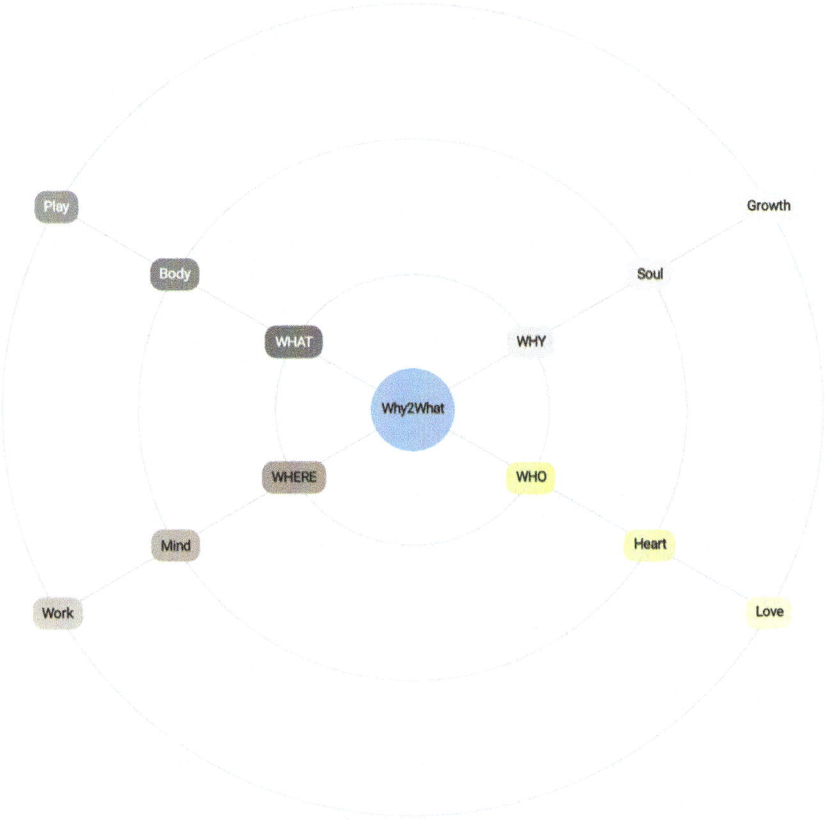

Fig. 4.1 MindMap Connected Choice constellations. The 4 dimensions (soul, heart, mind, body) and the 4 arenas of energy (growth, love, work, play) mutually influence each other. A snapshot of the connection between the 4 dimensions that compose our being, the 4 energy arenas that we spend our time in, and the 4 macro-questions (why, who, where, what) that derive from this constellation illustrate that everything is connected. The purpose that we identify as ours (Why) shapes our experiences and expressions (What) which influences our personality (Who) and the evolution of our life (Where)

Remaining acutely aware of the status quo is useful. When we notice over an extended period of time a discrepancy between our aspirations and actions it is time to assess whether an update of our dreams is overdue because our passion has shifted. Or, if the aspiration remains intact and yet the action is not in synch with it, asses which modifications of our course of action we must proactively initiate.

Assessing the status quo means to take stock, with candid honesty. The following tools are meant to help you sketch a snapshot of how you presently perceive your place, personality, and position in life; and to which extent a pro-active stance connects your aspirations and your actions. This stance is the link between your present (*Experiencing I*) and your desired future (*Being I*).

The 4 macro questions are a way to start that assessment. If you have not already done so, I suggest you put this book aside for a moment and jot down a couple of notes for each question. You may wish to complete them later (Tool-5), or explore them further (Tool-6).

*

TOOL-5 Visit the 4 macro-questions, and note down, uncensored by your inner watch-dog, what comes to your mind:

WHY do you **aspire** to live?
WHO do you **feel** you are?
WHERE do you **think** you are in your life?
WHAT do you **do** to align your aspirations and your actions?

*

TOOL-6 Plots for further digging:

- Are the 4 dimensions of your being (soul, heart, mind, body) addressed in each of the 4 energy arenas (growth, love, work, play) or are you compromising, and compensating to cope with gaps?
- Looking at the 4 energy arenas (growth, love, work, play) where do you see need for re-alignment?

In the table below (going from left to right and top down), look at each area of our life and mark which dimension/s are addressed in which arena/s. The empty spots may indicate space for re-alignment:

	Growth	Love	Work	Play
Aspiration				
Emotion				
Thought				
Sensation				

Revisit your answers from time to time, ideally at regular intervals. Your answers may evolve.

****

<u>Inner Interrogation utensils over time:</u>

The following complementary sequences can help us track our personal evolution over time:

Mini—(Behavior)—relating to the concrete manifestation of our values and wishes, or, the behavior to align our aspiration and action—WHAT am I doing in this moment, today?

Measured along short-term goals (e.g., daily or weekly) it offers a snapshot of our progress on the path that we envision. Possible questions:

Are my actions and aspirations aligned?
Does my behavior reflect the values that I admire?

Mezzo[3]—(Thoughts)—relating to our rational mindset regarding the status quo—WHERE do I stand?

Measured in regular intervals (e.g., monthly or biannually) it tracks milestones. Possible questions:

What is the current set-up of my life?
Am I engaged in the 4 energy arenas (growth, love, work, play) or am I neglecting one/several ones?

Midi—(Emotions)—relating to our emotional assessment of the status quo—WHO am I, right now?

Measured in regular intervals (e.g., annually, ideally combined with daily emotional check-ins, which may be combined with a moment of conscious self-time, a Me-Moment that is booked in the agenda of each day) it trains our awareness. Possible questions:

How do I feel about my Self?
How do I feel about my present situation?

Maxi—(Aspirations)—relating to our aspirational orientation—WHY am I (still) here?

Measured every year it serves as the larger playbook. By connecting the short-, medium-, and long-term aspirations that derive from our quest for meaning it serves as a reminder of that which matters (or mattered once) to us. Possible Questions:

Why am I here—in this place, this relationship, this line of work; in this life?
Have my goals changed—If Yes, is that because I lowered my standards or because I learned something about myself or the World that makes me want to adjust the course of my action?

****

4.2 Connecting the Dots

WHY we engage in something influences WHO we are which influences WHERE we stand in life now which influences WHAT we do in that space. Conversely, WHAT we do influences WHERE we are and move onto, and WHO we become, which may influence how we define our WHY in life. Our being and becoming is part of an organically evolving spectrum. Its course is shaped by our choices.

The POZE Paradigm, as presented in Chapter 1, has been illustrated through the stories in Chapters 2 and 3. Respectively and together our soul (Why), Heart (Who), Mind (Where), and Body (What) influence who we are, what we do, and thus who we become. Everything is connected; mind and matter, inside and outside. Nothing occurs in a vacuum. Regardless of where they live and come from, those who consciously seek the best interest of others end up benefiting from better quality of life, physically, mentally, and emotionally.[4]

Two patterns emerge from the stories in the previous pages; relating to Attitude and Mindset. The first could be summarized as *Purpose, Optimization, Zenith, and Exposure*; the second as *Perspective, Optimism, Zeal, and Excellence*. A couple of words on each as they may serve you in the review of your own approach to life and living.

The testimonials of those who shared their journey here are marked by 4 **Attitude** elements:

Purpose—the orientation towards meaning. Each of us can make a difference. Everyone has a unique combination of skills, assets, personality, and connections that enables us to make a unique contribution to society. If a person does not invest time to identify and pursue their own purpose—which may be a collection of different tasks that are connected by a common thread, then the mission that they could distinctively fulfill are distinctively placed to fulfill remains undone. Their own life and the World preserves a void. This void will hurt ever more as time goes by. Course corrections are possible at any point in time. Change begins by acknowledging the status quo.

Optimization—the quest to make internal and intrapersonal dynamics as smooth as possible. When our aspirations and actions are aligned our internal appreciation, and deriving from it our external appearance, are in synch. Communities can be tailored towards optimized energy flows, once the complementarity of every member is acknowledged and addressed.

Zenith—the ongoing pursuit of our own best self. The journeys of personal change and social transformation propel each other; taking the individual traveler and humanity altogether forward to the best version of itself, an organically evolving ZENITH. We may never reach the final stage; because once we attain what we had thought of as the ultimate goal, we find that new horizons and further vistas to pursue have arisen. Rather than one zenith, there are many; we grow to grow further, from one milestone to the next. Along the way we come ever closer to our highest self. As we learn more about ourselves our perspective on life changes; as mental filters and misperceptions dissolve.

Exposure—the conscious willingness to encounter reality as it is, not as we would like it to be; including our own nature. Deep down we know that there is more to life than survival; that being alive is not meant to be reduced to making a living. Facing this inner voice for more requires honesty with ourselves. Because when we compare what we aspire to with the actions that we engage in presently, discrepancies (may) appear. The latter can be ignored only for so long. Eventually, reality stares us in the face, and the later in life it is, the more challenging and painful it is to reverse course. Yet it remains possible until our last breath.

The presented journeys were influenced by a **Mindset** that entails 4 features:

Perspective—the ability to look at situations with the holistic understanding of connectedness and the acceptance of change. Everything evolves, and so do we. Once we acknowledge that life is a kaleidoscope that is continuously reassembling itself, it becomes easier to relinquish control, and accept the present with a learner's mind.

Optimism—the choice to search for the good in oneself, others, and situations. Even though we may have a natural predisposition towards a positive or a negative perception,[5] neither of these is engraved in stone or in our DNA. It is possible to train our mind to systematically look for the positive aspects in any given situation, based on the assumption that (almost) everything is or will eventually be good for something. For some people this comes naturally, for others it is a drastic shift in perspective. If it is pursued consciously and over time the synaptic connections in our brain adjust to this new way of thinking (Doidge 2008). Thus, eventually, conscious effort becomes a natural habit.

Zeal—the drive to move forward in the pursuit of life, with joy. Once we identify and commit to our purpose, we liberate the power that has been ours from the beginning. Energy flows when we invest ourselves in a goal that we passionately care about. If there is nothing that triggers that passion in your current life, than something is missing. It is important to distinguish passion that empowers, and desire that disempowers. The former frees us from external circumstances because it is fueled by the quest for a WHY that is bigger than our own interests; the latter makes us dependent on external clusters (Sect. 3.1) such as people, privileges, and material elements that are ultimately not under our control.

Excellence—the motivation to always give the best. Life evolves within a dynamic that does not contain judgement. Apparent opposites are complementary, and as we move on, we may gravitate from one end of the scale to the other. The only aspect of certainty in this is that we can choose to give our own best in any given situation, based on our best knowledge and skill set at that time. A stance that is challenging to adopt and appealing to accommodate is that of excellence without attachment. "Give your best and then let go," is a central principle of Karma Yoga. Once we relinquish our expectations regarding the outputs and outcomes of our behavior, we free energy and brain space to concentrate on the tasks at stake. When we invest our very best than we can accept whatever comes out with eased conscience.[6]

This book is part of an ongoing dynamic of connecting with the growing number of thinkers and doers whose attitude and mindset is marked by these elements. If you feel part of it, please reach out.

Thank You
Cornelia

Notes

1. Whatever we feel, think and do, is rooted in the craving for a purpose, the need to be part of something larger than ourselves (Frankl 1946). Once we are aware of this intrinsic motivation, we can systematically channel our time and energy to identify what that purpose of ours is. It is an essential part of personal evolution, because in the pursuit of our purpose we gradually find and unveil our best self. Furthermore, research has shown that contributing to a social cause is one of the best guarantees of longevity and life satisfaction (Harvard Second Generation Study 1990).
2. This process of the new overriding the old is supported by our neurological set-up. With new behavior new synapses are activated in the brain which overwrite the existing ones. With each repetition these new synaptic connections are strengthened. Conversely, continuing to repeat the preexisting habit strengthens the neurological underpinning of that behavior (Doidge 2007).
3. Moxy refers to the intermediate stage that is not yet half-way.
4. The previous books on POZE present the multidisciplinary foundation of this statement. Please refer in particular to Walther (2020) (see also Notes 1 and 2).
5. Although few studies have examined the genetic basis of optimism and pessimism, scholars generally provide heritability estimates of about a quarter for these traits. Heritability estimates for other personality traits such as extraversion and neuroticism are typically higher. Some psychologists believe this implies that heredity exerts an indirect influence on optimism and pessimism. For example, optimism may be influenced by the genes for extraversion and pessimism by the genes for neuroticism. An alternative explanation is that genetic factors directly influence the likelihood of success or failure. These experiences, in turn, stimulate the development of an optimistic or pessimistic explanatory style (Beck 1967). Environmental factors, in particular those encountered in childhood, also influencing a person's outlook (Peterson and Seligman 1984; see also Sapolsky 2004).
6. Whether the outcome is positive or not is not under our control. Accepting this disconnect between input and output is the foundation of karma yoga,

and of a serene life. Of the paths to spiritual liberation in Hinduism, karma yoga is the path of unselfish action (Raju 1954). It teaches that a spiritual seeker should act according to dharma ([in Indian religion] the eternal and inherent nature of reality, regarded in Hinduism as a cosmic law underlying right behavior and social order), without being attached to the fruits or personal consequences (Bhawuk 2011).

References

Beck, A. T. (1967). *Depression: Clinical, Experimental, and Theoretical Aspects*. New York: Harper & Row.

Bhawuk, D. (2011). *Spirituality and Indian Psychology: Lessons from the Bhagavad-Gita*. Springer Science, pp. 147–148 with footnotes. ISBN 978-1-4419-8110-3.

Doidge, N. (2007). *The Brain That Changes Itself: Stories of Personal Triumph from the Frontiers of Brain Science*. ISBN 978-0-670-03830-5 (hc.)/ISBN 978-0-14-311310-2 (pbk.).

Doidge, N. (2008). *The Brain That Changes Itself: Stories of Personal Triumph from the Frontiers of Brain Science*.

Frankl, V. (1946). *Men's Search for Meaning*. Republication by Paperback (2006).

Harvard Second Generation Study. (1990). Retrieved (February 2020) from www.adultdevelopmentstudy.org.

Peterson, C., & Seligman, M. E. (1984). Causal Explanations as a Risk Factor for Depression: Theory and Evidence. *Psychological Review*, Vol. 91, pp. 347–374.

Raju, P. T. (1954). The Concept of the Spiritual in Indian Thought. *Philosophy East and West*, Vol. 4, No. 3 (Oct., 1954), p. 210.

Sapolsky, R. M. (2004). *Why Zebras Don't Get Ulcers*. Chicago: Owl Book/Henry Holt and Co.

Walther, C. (2020). *Development, Humanitarian Aid and Social Welfare: Social Change from the Inside Out*. New York: Palgrave Macmillan.

Annexes

Annex A: Participating Storytellers

Destination unknown

Lee Kim, Global Congress Lead. Pfizer Innovative Health & Innovation
Born 1973. Jejudo, South Korea

A life along watershed decisions
Ulrich Hemel, Director WeltEthos Institut; Founder Institut for Sozial Strategy
Born 1954. Bensheim/Berggasse, Germany

Open to Explore
Marielle Sander, Representative United Nations Populations Fund (UNFPA) Papua New Guinea
Born 1964. Jönköping, Sweden

Better than I could have ever dreamt of
Christian Joerg, Co-Founder and Managing Partner | Ellis Accelerator
Born 1963. Munich, Germany

My North Star
Joan AI. Founder 'Prepared Child'
Born 1975. Shanghai, China

Legacies
Erastus Mong'are. Founder and CEO for StartUpAfrica Inc.

C. C. Walther, *Leadership for Social Change and Development*,
https://doi.org/10.1007/978-3-030-76225-4

Born 1971. Kisii County, Kenya

Follow your curiosity
Andi Cuddington, facilitator by day, kitchen dance party enthusiast by night, and traveler by heart
Born 1984, Vancouver, Canada

Purpose without action is daydreaming
John Roche, SAP Advisor
Born 1964. Providence, RI USA

My Life's Journey So far
Gareth Owen, Humanitarian Director of Save the Children UK
Born 1968, Kettering, England

Crises require change
Almuth von Below-Neufeldt. Retired member of the lower saxony state parliament
born 1954. Hamburg, Germany

Shifing by degrees
Randah Taher. Culture Designer and Innovation Facilitator
Born 1977. Arabo-Canadian

From Growth to Change to (m)Equilibrium
Andrew Shatte. Co-founder and Chief knowledge management officer mEquilibrium
Born 1962. Brisbane, Australia

Perpetual change
Ofri Hirsch. Soulkitchen Chef. US
Born 1975. Afula, Israel

Purpose Pursuit
Jaha Cummings. Councilman for the City of Punta Gorda
Born 1973 Coral Gables, Florida

Following Faith
Yunsun Chung, Primary investigator for 'Designing Food Revolution for Social Change'
Born 1964. Seoul. South Korea

Annex B: Graphic Overview—Dimensional Ratings

The following two graphics offer a snapshot of the dimensional ratings of participants. It should be noted that the number of participants in this sample was small. Further research is required (and ongoing) to corroborate the image that seems to emerge from this (Figs. B.1 and B.2).

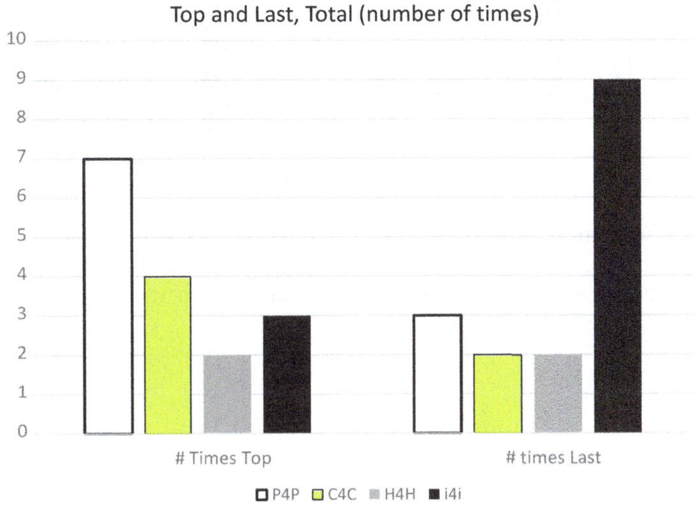

Fig. B.1 Aspiration to purpose (here referred to as P4P) was the most often identified as a compass for decision-making by the participants. The least selected one was the intended influence that derives from behaviour (i4i)

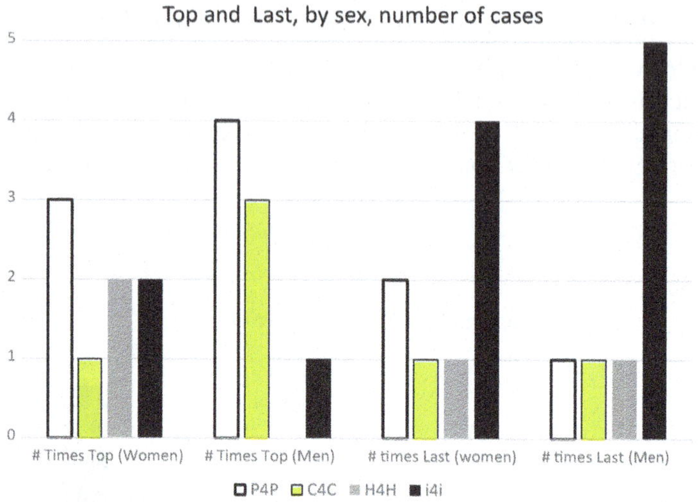

Fig. B.2 Aspiration to purpose (P4P) was ranked the highest by women and men. For women, the second dimensions most often ranked first were H4H and i4i but for men it was C4C. Influence through behaviour was the least rated one among men and women

Index

C. C. Walther, *Leadership for Social Change and Development*,
https://doi.org/10.1007/978-3-030-76225-4

D

E

G

The manufacturer's authorised representative in the EU is Springer
Nature Customer Service Centre GmbH, Europaplatz 3, 69115 Heidelberg,
Germany. If you have any concerns regarding our products, please
contact ProductSafety@springernature.com

Printed and bound by CPI Group (UK) Ltd, Croydon, CR0 4YY
30/09/2026
02225472-0013